TOP SECRET ECONOMIC INFORMATION
(This book is a compilation of many of my website essays. I'm sorry if there are any repeats of subject matter).

ECONOMIC RECOVERY BULL...

A minimum wage is like a vehicle with no reverse or an army walled of from any retreat. Getting rid of the minimum wage and cutting taxes to the bone will at least save the USA from total chaos and allow us to live and fight another day.

I0473664

Where do most citizen tax payers get their money, from their small business employers? Where do businesses get their money, from citizen customers, some of which they themselves employ. As you can see the economy operates as a giant cycle.

Human energy and intelligence creating something of value in the form of food and resources is what keeps this cycle going. And the rewarding byproduct of the whole process is what's called profit. That is what government takes, all taxes ultimately comes from some form of profit.

Sure, government needs a certain amount of profit driven tax money to protect the nation from both foreign and domestic enemies and basic interior needs. But, the USA government was never designed to be a cradle to grave social and family provider.

Now, big government at all levels is taking far too much of small businesses profit for many of them to survive let alone hire anyone. And you gonna tell me mass tax cuts to the bone is not the answer, go fly a kite!!!

STONE AGE.
Most people with common sense think the biggest threat to the survival of the USA is its financial crisis cause by big government spending. I don't think so, I think what is slowly driving the dagger in the heart of this great nation is what big government has done to our nuclear and extended family system.

No famine, financial collapse, nuclear attack, mass chemical attack, or mass biological attack can destroy this huge nation with our strong nuclear and extended family system along with our minimum bartering capacity is this statement true or false? Then you are the judge.

In terms of raw survival big government as the welfare state has destroyed everything and left us with a leadership in complete denial along with countless gimmy, gimmy, do for me dependents. Culture and survival wise just about the only option we have left is to regress back to the Stone Age unless our leaders snap out of denial and face cold steel rock hard reality.

Folks, I'm just a lowly lone writer telling it as I see it, pray that I'm wrong. Like a broken record I repeat, no one wants this but it would keep us from going back to the Stone Age. Get rid of the minimum WAGE and cut taxes to the bone across the board.

Then whatever income the government takes in should first go to national defense and administrative cost, and whatever is left go to community kitchens, hospitals, and shelters. Sure, its extreme but it is better than going back to the Stone Age. If anyone has a better solution they better step up now because I see the Stone Age over the horizon.

Everybody is all worked up over health care and socialism. But, unless my advice to get rid of the minimum wage and cut taxes to the bone is taken serious nothing is going to stop the USA and global economy from going back to the Stone Age.

Cost, cost, and more cost is the problem with health care and if the government thinks it can take it over and not pay the cost it will destroy medical care in America. However, it is going to take it over anyway if not today it will be tomorrow, because the only way to stop it would be to dismantle the welfare state and I'll leave it at that.

And the root reason why medical cost has

shot through the roof pass the sky is the limit into outer space is because government got into it in the first place. Anything the government gets into in a free country the cost will always go through the roof because government doesn't adhere to market force principals. Enough said.

As to capitalism versus socialism that is the least of our problems. No form of government can save a nation from doom if it looses its nuclear and extended family foundation, which we have. I know I keep writing the same thing over and over but if I can enlighten just one mover and shaker it will be worth it. Amen.

LATE ENTRY III: 20 OCTOBER 2009, 1335 HOURS.
IS IT DESTINY OR FROM A HIGHER POWER?

I, Freddie L. Sirmans, Sr. a shy neurotic uneducated south Georgia USA country boy is now teaching the world basic economics, somebody need to teach it. Ninety nine percent of the American people don't know what is actually powering this big USA and global economic ship.

Without this source power the whole USA and global economy will be left adrift. Almost everyone thinks its power comes from the government and the American tax payers.

That is a source but it is not the root source, plus almost all thinking stops there.

Very few probe deeper and discovers who is actually paying taxes to the government. And even those that do acknowledge that it is the business and working people of America, and that is the end of it.

American small businesses do employ far more people in this country than anything else so that must be the main source powering the USA economy. Well, I guess that's it we have an open and shut case.

Whoa, not so fast, I beg the difference, for the record I will prove that it is something called "Profit" that is the root source that powers the USA economy or any successful economy. We all need a certain amount of food and basic resources to live on. So, whatever amount over what we need to survive on is what's called extra or profit that we can exchange for money or whatever.

The accumulation of excess profit is what makes one rich or wealthy. A business is only a medium to exchange goods or services for a profit, no profit, no business, no employee, and nothing for the government to tax. Big government at all levels, federal, state, and local has put so many taxes, license fees, permit fees, rules, regulations, and other mandates on a business that it is a miracle anyone makes a profit.

Almost any blood sucking economic system will work for 80-100 years, then its hell to pay. This welfare state system is like a dog chasing its tail because a business is only a means of exchange; all cost must be passed on to the public which in turn raises the cost of living on everyone. I rest my case your honor.

The USA economy is now at the point it fits the old proverbial saying: "A straw broke the camels back."

LATE ENTRY II: 14 OCTOBER 2009, 0831 HOURS.
I once heard this story about a man with a mule that would walk about twenty yards or so stop briefly and continue on and on. Someone asked the owner what was the problem with this mule, why he acted like that?

The owner said the mule was afraid he might not hear the owners command so he stops to listen. Well, I think that same analogy can be applied to the liberals running this country.

They have all of the power and are almost totally in control of this great country. So, what is the problem with them, why are they acting the way they are? I ask why don't they just follow their own beliefs and convictions and stop all of this stopping for bipartisan support.

The fact is: The idea of taking on responsibility all alone with no one else on hand to shift blame to, scares the hell out of a liberal.

LATE ENTRY: 10 OCTOBER 2009, 1016 HOURS

The financial burden load of the welfare state has bankrupted this nation and sent our manufacturing and jobs over seas. But, that is not the worst thing the welfare state beast has done to this great predominate Christian nation.

The worst thing is it has ripped out the inner fabric of this great nation by destroying our nuclear and extended family system, and any capacity to barter; there is no recovery from this. Stone Age here we come. However, the future is never written in stone. Getting rid of the minimum wage and cutting taxes to the bone can still save us.

Getting rid of the minimum wage and cutting taxes to the bone, you must be crazy, of course that's not going to happen, and the power structure and big money will go down in flames first. If only enough common sense citizens would pledge to vote for people willing to get rid of the minimum wage and cut taxes to the bone this great predominate Christian nation would be saved.

* There is an old saying that: "If you say something long enough and loud enough eventually someone is going to believe you." Maybe not mine but some nation is going to believe me.

FREDDIE L. SIRMANS, SR'S LOG: 14 SEPTEMBER 2009, 1231 HOURS. RECOVERY, RECOVERY, BS!

My God! My God! Come on folks, economics ain't rocket science; a hundred and fifty years ago almost everyone knew what I keep telling people. It is not just the shallow minded liberals, hardly anyone anymore have a strong survival instinct.

Anyone that thinks the USA can continue to carry the financial burdens of our big government welfare state is either in complete denial or just plain ignorant. If you think I am a fool and nut case, you are wrong.

History has proven that it is always the masses that are wrong. I have the wisdom and survival instinct to know beyond a shadow of a doubt that I'm right, so help me God. However, reason never changes closed minds.

Very few people truly understand how an economy works as well as I do. Almost everyone think in term of big money, but it is not the amount it is the buying power that counts in the long run.

The other team can't run up the score if you got the ball. It is the same in economically terms; prices can't go above what the always larger poorer population can afford to pay. That is unless a big government welfare state unconstitutionally hands out free money on an individual basis.

That act subsidizes high prices, and is what feeds this never ending inflationary spiral that we are caught up in. Sure, you can help the poor, but you can't hand out cash and food stamps on an individual basis and not destroy the free market place price structure.

That is because there is just two teams the seller (merchants) and the Buyer (consumers). And the government is supposed to fill the role of referee and tax collector. However, that is no longer the case the government is taking tax money from one team and giving it to the other.

Mother Nature says hell no, that breaks nature's supreme law of "Natural selection;" and she is preparing to step in and create a rebirth by starving the whole system back to the Stone Age.

If the government was not hogging the free market place, the free market place would heal itself. Now, the only way to get this beast out of the market place is to starve it out, it has grown far too powerful. Otherwise, there is no way to keep the USA from starving to death in just a very few years, you mark my word.

In my view the USA and the global economy is in a state of mass denial. No one wants to face the cold steel rock hard reality. If I have to repeat it a thousand times, man cannot use figures and intelligence to manage a successful economy because the variables are infinite.

However, there is nothing complicated or secret about how to run a time tested successful economy. There is a proven time tested ideology that has never failed to produce far more food and goods than any one nation can consume.

That ideology is, "Allow free competition and let the free market work," it is just that simple. But no, today we have all of these learned economists that think they can out smart Mother Nature, wrong. It is like having a vehicle with no reverse, you can't have a free floating free market place economy with a minimum wage.

You can't have a lasting free market place economy when sky high taxes and every other kind of government mandate is siphoning off most of a business's profit. For a democracy to survive and last every individual and family unit must carry its own weight. I keep hearing about a recovery, that is BULLSHIT!

I can only speak for my self, but in my view it is impossible to have a recovery with all of the financial burdens our welfare state is now carrying, after years of adding more and more the load is just too much. Also, I believe unless the minimum wage is junked and taxes cut to the bone more and more businesses are going to fail with even higher unemployment.

Listen up! Profit, profit, profit, is everything; there will be nothing for the government to survive on itself if not enough business's is making enough profit to stay afloat.

The government can only tax a profitable business, no one making a profit, nothing for the government to tax because not even Joe public gets paid if he doesn't have a job, it's just that simple. Think about it.

According to the constitution the only financial burdens our federal government should be carrying is to protect the nation from foreign and domestic enemies and to finance a healthy interior department.

But, oh no, we gave the "New deal" a foot in the door and since then liberal politicians from both parties have created this welfare state beast that is determine to grab absolute power and take away our individual freedom.

I say hell no! This beast has taken on financial burdens galore even as small as a hangnail, all out of the hard earned profits of the barely hanging on large and small business men/women of America. I say, snap out of it learned economists, face reality; lets take our bitter medicine and go boldly into the future.

We can do all things through God which strengthens us, Phil. 4-13 paraphrased.

ECONOMIC LECTURE #15 by Freddie L. Sirmans, Sr.
High drama, stay tuned for the next episode

PS: The Super Great Thinker Rides Again!

FREDDIE L. SIRMANS, SR'S LOG: 19 JULY 2009, 1155 HOURS
A SUPER GREAT BRAIN STORMING HEALTH CARE IDEA!
This may sound radical and surprising coming from a die hard anti-big government

advocate like me. Seriously, do Americans really want health care fixed or not. Well, I'll tell you how, you may not agree or like it but it's the most safe and practical approach to our life or death health care problem that I've ever heard of.

First, responsible leadership should set up in several large cities a test system similar to the veterans system, but, keep it separate by using only a token like script. Next, issue the scrip to only those below a certain income or other qualifying conditions.

After about a year or so there should be some proven results one way or another, that way we may not destroy the best health care system to ever exist in the history of mankind. Note, I didn't say the cheapest, but it is by far the best in the world. If test results are positive, sure, it could be expanded.

Still, my belief is the only way to save the USA medical health care system or even the economy itself is to kick the government completely out of it, period. If the government insist on being uncle sugar then fund public only things off to the side, but don't destroy the nation's culture, economy, and everything else in the process.

When government is out of the way natural selection market forces will never let prices or anything else get out of control. "You can't get blood out of a turnip and a chain is only as strong as its weakest link." A business can't charge more than the poor can pay, that is if the government butt out mind its own business and let the nuclear family fulfill its proper role.

Economic lecture #8

GITMO AND WATER BOARDING!

For some reason those two subjects just won't get out of the limelight. For some reason the liberals just won't let go and let sleeping dogs lie. They just keep fueling the fire and boiling this dirty linen in public when matter like this should be settled at the highest levels behind closed doors.

I can't predict the future and no one can, but I think there is an even chance this sleeping dog may end up biting a bunch of liberals. When I turn on the TV all I hear is Gitmo, Gitmo, all day long. For me to meddle in an issues of this type is unpredictable and may even be dangerous, but, as a writer I just couldn't take it any longer, I just had to put pen to paper, so be it.

Now, here is my ounce of wisdom, you can take it with a grain of salt or you can take it to the bank. As I kick back in my recliner and listen to the liberals and others talk, the main thing they are focusing on is how secure the maximum security prisons are and that nobody has ever escaped.

They are not even in the ballpark on the danger of closing Gitmo and bringing those prisoners here. Of course, I'm not one bit surprised because I think most liberals are shallow and lack real wisdom. In fact it is not just the liberals, the welfare state has made nearly 90 percent of the American population shallow and hype prone, over a hundred million people voted for the American idol winner.

The mostly liberal media is so bias against anything conservative that they wouldn't tell you even if they did see a closing Gitmo threat, which they don't. Very few Americans actually see the big picture here. I may be wrong but I believe if Gitmo is closed and those people are brought here on American soil we will have a whole new ball game.

I believe this whole life or death struggle we are locked in will be ratcheted up several notches. Let's just say one member of a family clan is being held for whatever reason and the rest of the family members know where he is being held, do you think the rest of the family is going to forget him and stay far, far away?

No, we are dealing with people that has no

fear of death, and I will bet they will create moles and try to get as close as possible. I don't know what will happen and no on does but you can rest assured if you put those people here on American soil the sky will be the limit. I'm just one lone writer expressing my grave concerns.

Gitmo is on an island surrounded by water which makes it extremely hard to get to, plus it is not even our territory. But, all of that will change if you bring those people here on the North American mainland. If the ante is raised by bringing those people here on American soil, nothing may happen, but, we better be prepared to guard our malls and everything else like never before.

Folks, I'm a self-made writer and great thinker, I'm not even right half of the time, and I may be just making a mountain out of a mole hill. So, never mind me, just go on about your business and forget you even read this article. Phil. 4-13 I can do all things through God which strengthens me.

FREDDIE L. SIRMANS, SR'S LOG: 14 MAY 2009, 1215 HOURS

As I have said before a "Welfare State" is the most dangerous and destructive form of government to ever exist in the history of civilization. No other form of government exist that will completely rip the nuclear family system apart and make it impossible for that society to survive long term.

It destroys the sense of self-responsibility and accountability in people, it kills a strong survival instinct and lulls people into a love, love false sense of security, and then drives the final nail in by breeding people that is asleep and don't have the character or judgment to recognize a moral or any other threat until the wolf is at the door.

The following are the things every society must have to survive and it destroys every last one of them. There is very little left of our once strong nuclear and extended family system, especially among African Americans, you can now wipe the floor with our once strong morals and values code, and our once breadbasket Midwest small farmers along with the rest of the nation's small farmers and home gardeners that got us through the great depression is long gone.

We have almost no emergency fallback bartering capacity to keep this nation alive during a calamity. We as a people are at freedoms death door and it is so sad that still far too many people are more concerned about who is starring in Hollywood. I believe the government need to snap out of its denial, face reality and start planning how to survive through an inevitable collapse.

The nation needs to start planning masses of food kitchens, masses of food shelter programs, masses of medical clinics, and when that is completed junk the minimum wage and cut all taxes to the bone across the board. Then, the free market place will save itself and the country, too, if the government as designed will stays with protecting the country and let the economy sinks or swims on its own. No one wants this solution, but reality is reality.

This way, at least we will be in control, and even then we will have only a fighting chance to save our nation and freedom. Folks, I'm a writer and I write what I think and believe, no one has to believed me or take me serious. In truth, I, myself, hope I'm wrong on what I think.

Of course, I don't expect the powers that be to even consider a hard decision like this; they will continue to take the liberal course of least resistance. I expect the powers that be to make deals around the world and finish selling off what little is left of the soul of America.

FREDDIE L. SIRMANS, SR'S LOG: 13 MAY 2009, 1530 HOURS
A lot of good citizens look at the condition of America and wonder when and where did we go wrong. I, Freddie L. Sirmans, Sr. will tell

you when we the citizens lost control of this great country. It was around eighty years ago when we allowed the government to seize the traditional nuclear family provider role for itself.

You see, whoever is in the provider role is the boss and calls the shots. Instead of going into a lot of elaborating I will just get to the point. What started off initially as a small "New Deal" provider baby has over time grown into this huge monster size welfare state beast. Now the appetite of this ferocious beast is gobbling up every tax dollar or any other dollar that it can seize.

I believe it is futile and we are deluding ourselves to think we can save our economy and freedom as long as this beast is in the social and family provider role. This beast favors low values and loose morals and sees self-sufficiency as a threat to its power and that will not be tolerated.

We have this beast loose upon the land with unlimited taxing power, and that means no one in this country is safe from unreasonable taxes. Unless this beast is neutered and downsized out of its super provider role I think trying to save the economy and the country is a waste of time and resources. God save America.

BOOK SELLING WORLD SHUNS FREDDIE L. SIRMANS, SR'S BOOKS

I don't know how it is done, but, I believe the book selling world has an unwritten rule that prevents books by an extreme conservative neurotic like me from being sold. I can't prove it but I feel there may be a hidden hand somewhere preventing me from selling more books. Sure, some of the grammar is crude and incorrect to some degree; still the people should make that choice.

I believe a super great thinker and writer like me deserve to be selling books in the thousands. Now! Take that unwritten rule! Invisible hand! The name Freddie L. Sirmans, Sr. is out there, it is all over the internet. No one can convince me that there is not an opposing force that doesn't want it known what is in Freddie L. Sirmans' Books.

If nothing else, someone is going to buy just to see what is going on. Just because I'm saying it doesn't mean nothing is there. Just because someone is paranoid doesn't mean they are not in danger. Believe it or not, paranoid people live longer. There is no one alive today that better articulates in simple terms the inner working of how an economy should work.

I lay it out so simple that even an idiot can understand it. However, history has proven that one of the hardest things there is is to keep a genuine good man down. There is a destiny reason why a poor neurotic uneducated South Georgia USA country boy can reach out and grab the imaginary reins of the U.S. Economy, yank back and yell "Whoa" before it goes over the cliff. Praise be to God. Amen.

A word of knowledge to any conservative with his head above the crowd, the liberals may come after you with extra venom because of misplaced aggression. I'm the wanted target but that is out of the question. No liberal is going to make famous in their minds a nobody neurotic nut case. I have no hate or dislike for liberals in fact I think they are great Americans, but shallow and shouldn't control our destiny.

I consider myself a realist not a conservative. I love my country and as long as I have the freedom to write my views I'm going to say what I believe to be best for the long term survival of my country. I believe great character and good judgment goes hand in hand. And I believe great or good character can only come from some form of real or imposed struggle in life.

It is not just the liberals that lack the character to make sound judgment; we can't put all of the blame for the destruction of our culture and nuclear family system on them. I may be screwed up and unknown, but the liberals know I'm a deadly threat because I am striking at the heart of their false God, the "Welfare State." And in their eyes anyone that does that with a wallop is a mortal enemy.

I keep pounding body blows to their soft underbelly and sooner or later it's going to tally. The liberals know this and are counter punching by going after any high profile conservative they can sink their teeth in. This misdirected aggression is only going to increase. They won't dare focus attention on me because they feel the less people know what I'm writing the better.

My writing is based on logic and common sense and just like the saying goes, "The proof of the pudding is in the eating. And in this case the proof of the writing is in the reading." Throughout nature and survival there will always be an exception to everything. Having said that, anyone with genuine sound character and judgment will by instinct know that abortions and gay marriages are a threat to long term survival.

Exceptions are part of nature and those that are affected should be loved and respected, but a spade is a spade no matter what political correction says. I will say that less than five percent of the entire U.S. Population has the judgment today to even believe how close this nation is to total destruction as a free people. I have no need or desire to try to scare anyone, but as a writer I have a duty to share my wisdom and knowledge if it will help save this great nation.

I see a dire future, but the future is never set in stone, man always has the ability to determine his own future by his own actions.

PS: We have here high drama, stay tuned. You don't want to miss anything.

FREDDIE L. SIRMANS, SR'S LOG: 29 MAY 2009, 0829 HOURS
ECONOMICS WORDS OF AUTHORITY!!!

I say this with authority! And I'm speaking with great authority! By whose authority you speak, mine, my very own. Who gave you any authority, except, maybe being a nut case? Anyway, the fact remains, anyone that reads enough of my writing will know that I have super natural wisdom, case closed.

The government still doesn't get it. And ninety five percent of the nation's population still doesn't get it. The days of our welfare state as a super social and nuclear family provider is over. They were over twenty five years ago but the mostly liberal government policy chose instead to sell our soul and bankrupt the nation, now, the last of our world war II giant's head is on the chopping block.

Starting with the "New Deal" baby, now our monster size welfare state beast has destroyed our culture, our almost completely free market place, and is now taking over our private businesses. When masses of people surrender their independency to anything or anybody they have no authority left.

The federal government seized the social and nuclear family provider role for itself and we accepted and saw no threat at the time, now, it is almost too late. The government created the masses of poor welfare and other dependents. Now, it has a survival responsibility at all cost to provide community shelters, kitchens, and medical clinics for these folks.

In closing, I'm going to lay out the cold steel facts with authority! Nothing! And I mean nothing, is going to save the California or the United States economy except mass across the board tax cuts to the bone. That is it in a nut shell. No one is forced to believe me or take me serious; still, I speak with authority. Glory be to God, Amen.

Signed Freddie L. Sirmans, Sr.

PS: One thing is for sure, I may be neurotic and screwed up for life, but my wisdom and deep thinking is definite not common or ordinary by any means; it is a gift from God.

FREDDIE L. SIRMANS, SR'S LOG: 14 MAY 2009, 1215 HOURS

As I have said before a "Welfare State" is the most dangerous and destructive form of government to ever exist in the history of civilization. No other form of government exist that will completely rip the nuclear family system apart and make it impossible for that society to survive long term.

It destroys the sense of self-responsibility and accountability in people, it kills a strong survival instinct and lulls people into a love, love false sense of security, and then drives the final nail in by breeding people that is asleep and don't have the character or judgment to recognize a moral or any other threat until the wolf is at the door.

The following are the things every society must have to survive and it destroys every last one of them. There is very little left of our once strong nuclear and extended family system, especially among African Americans, you can now wipe the floor with our once strong morals and values code, and our once breadbasket Midwest small farmers along with the rest of the nation's small farmers and home gardeners that got us through the great depression is long gone.

We have almost no emergency fallback

bartering capacity to keep this nation alive during a calamity. We as a people are at freedoms death door and it is so sad that still far too many people are more concerned about who is starring in Hollywood. I believe the government need to snap out of its denial, face reality and start planning how to survive through an inevitable collapse.

The nation needs to start planning masses of food kitchens, masses of food shelter programs, masses of medical clinics, and when that is completed cut all taxes to the bone across the board. Then, the free market place will save itself and the country, too, if the government as designed will stays with protecting the country and let the economy sinks or swims on its own. No one wants this solution, but reality is reality.

This way, at least we will be in control, and even then we will have only a fighting chance to save our nation and freedom. Folks, I'm a writer and I write what I think and believe, no one has to believed me or take me serious. In truth, I, myself, hope I'm wrong on what I think.

Of course, I don't expect the powers that be to even consider a hard decision like this; they will continue to take the liberal course of least resistance. I expect the powers that be to make deals around the world and finish selling off what little is left of the soul of

America.

FREDDIE L. SIRMANS, SR'S LOG: 13 MAY 2009, 1530 HOURS

A lot of good citizens look at the condition of America and wonder when and where did we go wrong. I, Freddie L. Sirmans, Sr. will tell you when we the citizens lost control of this great country. It was around eighty years ago when we allowed the government to seize the traditional nuclear family provider role for itself.

You see, whoever is in the provider role is the boss and calls the shots. Instead of going into a lot of elaborating I will just get to the point. What started off initially as a small "New Deal" provider baby has over time grown into this huge monster size welfare state beast.

Now the appetite of this ferocious beast is gobbling up every tax dollar or any other dollar that it can seize. I believe it is futile and we are deluding ourselves to think we can save our economy and freedom as long as this beast is in the social and family provider role.

This beast favors low values and loose morals and sees self-sufficiency as a threat to its power and that will not be tolerated. We have this beast loose upon the land with unlimited taxing power, and that means no one in this country is safe from unreasonable taxes.

Unless this beast is neutered and downsized out of its super provider role I think trying to save the economy and the country is a waste of time and resources. God save America.

BOOK WORLD SHUNS FREDDIE L. SIRMANS, SR'S BOOKS

I don't know how it is done, but, I believe the book selling world has an unwritten rule that prevents books by an extreme conservative neurotic like me from being sold. I can't prove it but I feel there may be a hidden hand somewhere preventing me from selling more books.

Sure, some of the grammar is crude and incorrect to some degree; still the people should make that choice. I believe a super great thinker and writer like me deserve to be selling books in the thousands. Now! Take that unwritten rule! Invisible hand! The name Freddie L. Sirmans, Sr. is out there, it is all over the internet.

No one can convince me that there is not an opposing force that doesn't want it known what is in Freddie L. Sirmans' Books. If nothing else, someone is going to buy just to see what is going on. Just because I'm saying it doesn't mean nothing is there. Just because someone is paranoid doesn't mean they are not in danger. Believe it or not, paranoid people live longer.

There is no one alive today that better articulates in simple terms the inner working of how an economy should work. It is laid out so simple that even an idiot can understand it. However, history has proven that one of the hardest things there is is to keep a genuine good man down.

There is a destiny reason why a poor neurotic uneducated South Georgia USA country boy can reach out and grab the imaginary reins of the U.S. Economy, yank back and yell "Whoa" before it goes over the cliff. Praise be to God. Amen.

A word of knowledge to any conservative with his head above the crowd, the liberals may come after you with extra venom because of misplaced aggression. I'm the wanted target but that is out of the question. No liberal is going to make famous in their minds a nobody neurotic nut case.

I have no hate or dislike for liberals in fact I think they are great Americans, but shallow and shouldn't control our destiny. I consider myself a realist not a conservative. I love my country and as long as I have the freedom to write my views I'm going to say what I believe to be best for the long term survival of my country.

I believe great character and good judgment goes hand in hand. And I believe great or good character can only come from some form of real or imposed struggle in life. It is not just the liberals that lack the character to make sound judgment; we can't put all of the blame for the destruction of our culture and nuclear family system on them.

I may be screwed up and unknown, but the liberals know I'm a deadly threat because I am striking at the heart of their false God, the "Welfare State." And in their eyes anyone that does that with a wallop is a mortal enemy. I keep pounding body blows to their soft underbelly and sooner or later it's going to tally.

The liberals know this and are counter punching by going after any high profile conservative they can sink their teeth in. This misdirected aggression is only going to increase. They won't dare focus attention on me because they feel the less people know what I'm writing the better.

My writing is based on logic and common sense and just like the saying goes, "The proof of the pudding is in the eating. And in this case the proof of the writing is in the reading."

Throughout nature and survival there will

always be an exception to everything. Having said that, anyone with genuine sound character and judgment will by instinct know that abortions and gay marriages are a threat to long term survival.

Exceptions are part of nature and those that are affected should be loved and respected, but a spade is a spade no matter what political correction says. I'm an example, I'm screwed up for life, but, do that make me less of a human being, no, am I losing any sleep over it, no, but I do bleed, feel pain, and have feeling just like anyone else.

I will say that less than five percent of the entire U.S. Population has the judgment today to even believe how close this nation is to total destruction as a free people. I have no need or desire to try to scare anyone, but as a writer I have a duty to share my wisdom and knowledge if it will help save this great nation.

I see a dire future, but the future is never set in stone, man always has the ability to determine his own future by his own actions.

PS: We have here high drama, stay tuned. You don't want to miss anything.

THE THREE LECTURES BELOW BY THE SUPER GREAT THINKER FREDDIE L.

SIRMANS, SR. MAY GO DOWN IN HISTORY FOR SAVING THE U.S. ECONOMY.

Lecture #1

as a great thinker; let me Freddie L. Sirmans, Sr. give another short lecture on the basics of how an economy actually works. The solution to solving the auto industry's problems is very simple, cut all taxes to the bone and get government the hell out of the way. That is the only thing that is going to save the auto industry or the entire economy.

Our biggest problem concerning the economy is hardly anyone understands how a free market economy is supposed to work anymore, not even learned economist. I will try to make this lecture as simple as possible. Point #1: The government is not part of the economy and will never be able to run a successful economy. In economically terms the government is a parasite that is needed for protection of the whole society.

However, most governments have a different take on the matter, and also have the guns and the power to have its way. Point #2: The government can't run an economy because there are too many variables. A law of nature is the thing that runs a successful economy. This law was first recognized by Darwin many, many years ago. It is the law of "Natural selection."

A simpler definition is the process of "Supply and demand." The seller is the supplier and the buyer is the demand. Also, the seller is the same as merchant and the buyer is the same as consumer. That said, there are only two parties that make up an economy no matter how modern and advanced we are today, they are the seller and the buyer. The reward of profit is the only thing that drives an economy.

Also, great profit is what creates great wealth. Great wealth cannot be created in a nation without people willing to take great risk. And no one is going to be willing to take great risk without the expectation of making great profits. Let me do a walk through example: This farmer grows enough food for him and his family to survive on plus a little extra that he can use to barter or sell for a profit.

This farmer want to be come wealthy but he alone can only produce just a little extra to sell for a profit. He decides if he wants to become rich he must make much more profit. In order to make more profit he decides to hire a helper, but, out of that extra profit he must pay his hired helper first and only what is left is his profit. He is now a business man and he can keep hiring more help as long as he pays them first and have enough profit left over to make it all worth while.

Now, when the government comes in and demands a little cut it may not damage the system. But, when the government starts demanding almost the whole pie and the business man is no longer making a profit that is a horse of a different color. That is what causes people to loose jobs. That is where we are today, the welfare state tax load is just too heavy and without severe tax cuts the whole system is going to collapse, there is no doubt in my mind.

The welfare state in its provider role is standing between the seller and the buyer and as a parasite is siphoning off almost all of the sellers profit. With no profit it will soon be every man for himself and nobody producing any jobs. That is why if taxes are not soon cut to the bone its going to be impossible to save the auto industry or the U.S economy.

Beginning with the "New deal" our welfare state started off small but now after eighty years the tax bite has reached a saturation point and now it is cut taxes to the bone or back to the Stone Age. As I have said before there will be no safety latch great depression. Our welfare state has destroyed the infrastructure to support that, we no longer have a strong culture and moral code in place; we no longer have a necessary nuclear and extended family system, and we have almost no emergency fallback bartering capacity with small farmers and home gardeners.

When this economy collapses we face total chaos and possibly back to the Stone Age, there is no doubt about that. Point #3: A healthy economy must have a boom and bust cycle to get rid of the build up of moral and all kinds of inefficiency and decay. That is why no economy can be healthy without a strong nuclear and extended family system. A time may come when if you don't work you don't eat. Then the family and extended will be there for those too young, too old, too sick, or whatever to carry their share of the load. Sorry I went longer than planned. Class dismiss!

Today, April 10, 2009.
After around eighty years the United States welfare state economy has finally reached a saturation point. Class I will try to keep this lecture very short and not become long winded. However, I keep hearing these so called experts talking about a recovery and getting back to business as usual, I say poppycock, I totally disagree.

I believe our only chance of survival is draconian tax cuts. From a wisdom point of view every economy must sooner or later face a bust or rebirth cycle, it is a law of nature. People with money and power will never willingly accept the bust side of the "Boom and bust" cycle because for obvious reasons, they may lose everything.

However, it is going to happen sooner or later no matter what man does. It is a law of nature. It is the only way Mother Nature has of getting rid of waste, inefficiency, crud, moral decay and every other kind of anti-survival threat. Otherwise, anti-survival threats would become too powerful for mankind to exist.

Just look around to where we are headed moral and culture wise, we are headed off the chart and no law is gonna stop it. Now, let's turn to the greatest danger and threat to Western civilization that exist today, the "Welfare state." And even worse very few have the wisdom to see it. In my view no form of government has ever existed that is as dangerous as a welfare state.

It is like a sleeper; all the while it is eating and rotting away the inner core of a nation's very means of existing and almost everyone seems to be asleep like nothing matters. It is a system of winner take all, it will leave almost nothing in place to reorganize on to survive as a people.

You hear me mentioning the stone age a lot, well, when you have no culture with a strong moral code left, when you have no strong nuclear and extended family system left, and no emergency bartering capacity left, then you have no where else to go but back to square one, the stone age.

Lastly, let me walk through what happened to this still great nation that began with the "New deal." The intention was to do good by helping the poor. However, the liberals seized the opportunity to grab power and hold on to it and they did for forty years. But, my God! What a Cost! We are done, cooked!

It created this welfare state that snatched the social and family provider role from the traditional family head of household, without carrying out the hands on discipline that instilled self-restraint and respect for authority in young black men. That is why California blacks make up nearly 80 percent of the prison population and only around 5 percent of the general population.

The welfare state forced businesses our job providers to finance its super family provider role out of their profits. This act caused businesses to have to raise their prices to survive. When businesses were forced to raise their prices it raised the cost of living on everyone.

By government becoming a super family provider and giving out money on an individual basic that created a large enough pool of people with the money to keep price raising merchants in business, thereby pushing the cost of living up even higher. As the cost of living goes up, the government needs more and more tax money to support its ever growing provider role.

The whole thing created this vicious inflationary spiraling we have today, where businesses need to keep raising prices to make a profit and government need to keep raising taxes to support its super provider role. Sorry folks, I wanted to keep this lecture a lot shorter, but it is just too much going on. Class dismiss.

April 15, 2009
I, Great thinker Freddie L. Sirmans, Sr. decided to give this short lecture on government spending. I will try to make it as short and to the point as possible. I keep hearing so many public figures saying that almost all economists believe increasing government spending is good for the economy during a recession.

I totally disagree with that, I don't buy it for one second. Sure, if it means cutting taxes to the bone and spending to establishing government shelters, government kitchens, and hospitals, yes. Well, I may be the one that is the fool, but I believe mass increased government spending is a foolish idea.

I believe the main problem with the economy today is hardly anyone truly understands how a free market is suppose to work, most of the general public doesn't even have a clue. The only sure way is to go back to the very beginning with a group of people bartering and learn from there. All of these Wall Street inventions are just policy with procedures that only they truly understand.

The big question that matters is what creates wealth? The following is what the great thinker believes, me. I figured excess profit is what creates great wealth. And excess profit cannot be created without first risking an investment. Further, no nation can become rich and wealthy without a lot of people willing to take an investment risk.

Rule one is almost no one is going to be willing to take a great investment risk without first the expectation of a great profit reward, too high taxes diminishes that reward. The more government increases taxes and spending the less profit is going to be left for the businessman. To stay in business a business must make a profit, otherwise the business is history.

Increase government taxing and spending forces a business to raise its price to keep making a profit, thereby raising the cost of living on all of the people. Everything about a free market economy runs on profit. No profit, no risk takers, no risk takers, no wealth for the government to tax and spend. No profit is the reason all non free market economies remain dirt poor.

I believe there is a saturation point for rising taxes and our welfare state may have reached it. Just look around you the cost of living is leaving almost everyone broke. Most people simply don't have the money anymore to buy major items like new cars. And credit cards are making many people debt slaves.

Something gotta give, you can't get blood out of a turnip, and you can't have wealth to tax without a lot of people making a lot of profit. Lastly, how to run a successful free market economy? There are simply too many variables for the government to ever run a successful free market economy, intelligence, charts, figures, and all of that stuff is practically useless.

Allow free competition and let the free market place work is an ideology that has produced abundance of everything time and time again. However, hands off is a lot easier said than done for government, government is all about rewarding its friends and punishing it enemies.

I believe the idea of increased government spending during a recession is a liberal state of denial to hold on to power even if the country goes to hell. I really tried to keep it as short as possible. Class dismiss.

From the desk of Freddie L. Sirmans,Sr.
February 07, 2005
I. Survival Basics:
I, Freddie L. Sirmans, Sr. Decided to rant and vent on the subject of survival basics.
First, I will set the table and then get into the meat of the subject. I'm not going to be too concern about focus, I will probably be all over the map.

Caution:
Stop reading now, or read at your own risk, because I'm going to "Let her rip." I'm going to call it as I see it and let my thoughts just flow. You can call it "No holds barred, shooting from the hip" or some other metaphor because I'm fixing to deliver the cold steel rock hard buck naked facts as I see them. The time has past for tender feel good talk. After listening to the latest on a call in talk show concerning minor budget cuts I realized that this nation is in more serious trouble than even I could image.

With the rage I heard from folks calling in it seemed that reason has "Flew the coop". The way I see it is sane men and women must be able to disagree on solving our nation's budget problems, the government doesn't have an endless supply of money. The liberals have been more successful than they even realize.

After over seventy years they have succeeded in instilling a socialist mentality in close to ninety five percent of the American population to some degree. Nearly ninety five percent of the American population probably doesn't know what the basics of human survival are. We as a nation have a death wish and don't even know it. Sure, I understand that it is easy to tolerate cuts if the cuts don't affect you.

But, for the sake of the country we all need to be prepared to suck it up and move on with a positive attitude, we are still the freest country on earth with unlimited opportunities. The death wish I was speaking of is there are far too many self centered dependents that would rather see the whole system collapse than make a sacrifice. I'm scared, folks. We are in far more trouble than we think. Nothing will surprise me anymore.

Chasing a falling star or a pot of gold at the end of the rainbow, the nation may even vote the liberals back in power, which I believe will guarantee a total collapse. Sure, many already think I'm a kook, a far right nut, and out of touch, so be it, I'm not going to let up, I'm just getting warm. I don't play; I quit school because they had recess. When it gets so tough the chaplain goes AWOL that's when it's just getting comfortable for me.

Folks, this is not a game, we are playing for all of the survival marbles. I feel I have above average wisdom, but for God sake folks, most of this stuff is just plain common sense. Why have our learning institutions failed us so much? Maybe, "The death of common sense" did take place. The way I think and write is the way most people a hundred years ago took for granted.

Back then people knew what the basics of survival were and knew certain things don't ever change. Like everyone, I appreciate modern technology and all of the modern creature comforts, but I never forget that life is a cycle. Folks, I hope I'm wrong about what I think we are headed for. Sometimes I get so tired of ranting and shouting to deaf ears, ain't nobody listening. But, I just remember that "To more is given more is expected", I must continue on, the stakes are too high.

There will be no tomorrow or a second chance; it is my destiny to get the word out. Where is our survival instinct as a nation? What happen "To sometimes giving up a right for a wrong? Why are so many Americans Ignorant of how a free market place should work? Why, why folks, was a shy neurotic poor uneducated South Georgia country boy chosen to explain the obvious? Why Lord, why do I see and understand the solution so clearly when so many are caught up in this insane political correctness nonsense?

Why, why oh Lord was I given this awesome heavy burden? Wake up America. Praise the Lord. I won't look back. I wash my hands. In football as in all sports a winning coach will tell you "It's all about the basics". It's the same way with the economy and the survival of our country. The basics of survival as I understand is "It is the responsibility of the nuclear family or families to provide its own food, shelter, and warmth, plus, the responsibility of parents to care for their own children and the responsibility of grown children to care for their own elderly parents." That is it in a nut shell, everything else is gravy and icing on the cake.

Ninety five percent of Americans either don't know this or have forgotten it. Sure, it is good to have money, modern technology, and all of the fine creature comforts, but none of these things are going to save this nation if we are too far away from the basics. Most people especially the young think it is the responsibility of the government to take care of people that is fine; I don't have a problem with that. But, I'm one that knows that no government will last forever; all governments will go broke sooner or later.

Then, if you are too for away from the basics you have no foundation left to reorganize and rebuild upon, that is judgment day. When one grows old and can no longer work to earn their keep it is the primary responsibility of their offspring to care for them. The only exception is when the elderly have enough savings or other means of support. The reason why the economy is distorted and prices are growing further and further out of reach is because when government gives money to the people it subsidizes high prices and keep prices high.

In time it screws everything up. Without government subsiding high prices the free market place would bring prices down to the masses level and the poor would be able to pay their own way including medical bills. Plus, it would save our moral and family values by purging out most of today's societal problems. How we got away from the basics is when government became a daddy, the great white father provider.

Nature's supreme law of natural selection and survival is based on "need." I will guarantee you that we are doomed as a free country unless the social program swamp is dealt with. You will never be able to solve the illegal drug problem, the illegal immigration problem, or any other social problem unless you deal with the supply and demand that is driving it. The decline of America's nuclear family and social structure begin when government with good intentions slowly begin providing for family and social needs.

On the surface that doesn't seem like a bad thing and on a temporary basis it's not. But, it is the nature of things to grow, and given time it was a poison pill because it eliminates the survival need for the nuclear family. The destruction of the nuclear family is at the core of every social ill we have today. The nuclear family is the foundation of every civilization known to man and when it goes so goes western culture and civilization.

Illegal immigration and other social ills are only symptoms of the core problem, the destruction of our nuclear family and moral values, caused by the government playing sugar daddy. A certain amount of pain and suffering is part of life, and is the responsibility of the nuclear family, extended family, religious organizations, and the community. The government should stay with what it does best, that is, collect taxes and provide internal and external defense.

It should never get involve in the social arena except as a last resort on a temporary basis because government disrupts the free market place and the need for male head of households. Make no mistake about it, nothing less than privatizing almost all social programs are going to save this great, great nation, and probably all of western civilization with the global economy. But, I refuse to lose faith that America will do what has never been done before in the history of civilization, that is, reverse a course headed to a complete moral and economical collapse.

A cold hard fact is, no matter what I say or what the government does its going to go against someone's self interest, wisdom dictates that you do what benefits the most without abusing the few.

How did our circuit of existence come about?

The other day I was listening to this commentator and he asked something to this effect, "Can you prove that we are not the most intelligent beings in the universe." I thought about that and decided to ponder the question. I'm not sure if I or anyone can prove it but I know there is a higher power, you can call him God, A superior being, or whatever. You see, we are in a mental box called logic. We are locked in and cannot escape.

With only logic we will never be able to understand the beginning of our existence or our purpose here on earth. Our five senses connects us to reality, otherwise there would be no reality. Do that mean there would still be reality if no life could sense it? Like the old question: "If a tree fell in the Forrest and there were nothing or no body there to hear it, would there be a sound?" Who knows, in time other senses could evolve to produce a higher level of intelligent.

There are animals that have senses that can match almost anything we can do with modern technology and probably countless other things we haven't discovered and are not aware of. There are animals that have senses of radar, sonar, electricity, and many other things that modern technology can and cannot do. Who knows, there may be infinite worlds and dimensions coexisting with us that we don't have the senses to detect.

Who knows how Nessie and Bigfoot come and goes. In most of the animal world smell is the dominant sense and is many, many times more powerful than ours. Down wind a polar bear can smell prey almost a hundred miles away. It is almost unbelievable what a blood hound can do with the sense of smell. Logic dictates that there must be a beginning to everything. Just think of the old riddle, "Which came first, the chicken or the egg?"

Being boxed in with logic we can't even solve a simple little riddle like that. But, we know the answer must lie somewhere. We understand relativity, nothing don't just happen with no connection. In closing, wise men realized long ago that our power to reason was limited, so for the sake of sanity there must be a deity or deities with all the answers. I totally agree. Wait, hold on a moment, I've decided to delve deeper into this chicken and egg riddle.

Actually there is no such thing as which came first in the "Which came first, the chicken or the egg riddle." The chicken or the egg riddle is actually a life cycle circuit which is a unit of one. No matter how many parts a circuit has it still operates as one unit. My observation of the unit of one, oneness opens up far deeper questions, but I will leave it there for now.

Sure, life can evolve and adapt, but, a beginning life cycle circuit must be made, powered, maintained, and exist for some purpose. We humans don't make electrical circuits without some purpose.

From the desk of Freddie L. Sirmans, Sr. Nov. 04, 2004

For some reason I have an urge to write about the great depression that happen back in the early nineteen thirties. The first thing is I think we can forget about a depression happening in this country. That option has been taken always from us because of our big government provider role. I think what we are going to face is something that is much, much worse.

I think what we are headed toward is chaos and total collapse if we don't wake up as a nation. I don't think any government should ever take on a long term role as a provider, period. We have created something on a mass scale that has never happen in the history of mankind. We have lulled ourselves into a false sense of security on a mass scale. Never have so many people become almost totally dependent on a provider government with a vanishing nuclear family structure and no strong moral code intact as a security blanket.

Without these protections in place when faced with hunger and other survival struggles we could turn on one another and the expression "Dog eat dog" will be an under statement. With the whole world's unquenchable thirst for oil and all kinds of terrorist and economical threats out there, a severe calamity could hit any moment. Just think about it, what would happen if our economy collapsed. Huh, most people will look at you like you are a kook, because most people in this land of mass big government dependency is asleep.

Just like a little kid will think milk and eggs comes only from the grocery store, most people think the government can't go broke because it will always be able to squeeze another dollar out of tax payers. Not true, the government can and will go broke or make money worthless by flooding the economy with worthless money. In my view we have gotten too far away from the basics, our food supply and almost everything else has become mass produced, centralized, and trucked long distance.

All of this requires oil; oil has almost become the nation's only life blood we can't survive without mass supplies. If for whatever reason the government couldn't make it payroll, there is no backup plan to survive in this country without money. If a depression did hit us we would zoom right pass it to the next stage because people would be rioting in the streets. The people would have no means of surviving without their checks.

The government would have no choice but to print worthless money to buy time. But, after about three months of printing worthless money it would have no value. With money being worthless there may not be any dependable law enforcement. During emergencies we depend almost entirely on paid caretakers. Well, what would happen if money is worthless and there is no pay? Huh, you haven't thought about it, but in a struggle to survive nothing should be ruled out.

With our nuclear family in shambles and our moral and family values at it lowest there is nothing to stop us from going for each others throats. It could mean the survival of the meanest and the baddest; it could mean every man for himself. Anybody with real wisdom in this country knows that big government dependency is eventually going to destroy this country but politically don't know how to do anything about it.

True wise men and women have long realized we should dismantle big government to save our culture, but like I know it's not going to happen. I hate to admit it but we are past the stage of no return we all are too government dependent. In the eyes of nature our circumstance is normal because for a country to survive long term, rebirths must take place every so often. Just look at our economy, almost everything is out of balance.

People can't pay their bills. People are in debt way over their heads. Still, there are many people rolling in dough. Just look at the tax system, it is a disgrace, still, I get suspicious anytime they start talking about simplifying the tax system because in the past it always ended up in worse shape. I'm one that doesn't buy this idea that the poor or low income shouldn't pay income taxes. I think everyone should pay their fair share even if it's not but a penny.

I think we should have a system where everyone pays a flat rate at a fixed percentage with an ascending sir charge rate table for upper income levels. Also, provide an ascending discount rate table for the poor and low income, no deductions and excuses for anyone, period. All one would need to do was look at the rate chart and fill in four or five blanks spaces, done. Also, I have enough faith in the American people to believe they would still support their favorite charity.

That way everybody would pay something, no one would go Scott free. The rich could no longer escape through tax shelters. Plus, like it is now, why should the poor care about income tax increases, they don't have an investment in the system; someone else is caring the load. The poor always seem to find a way to play the lottery, why not make a small investment in their own country. After all, their votes cancel out tax paying votes. Sure, its tough love but I'm one that doesn't believe in pampering anyone.

You never let the poor drown but the fact is you only help the poor by forcing them to try to help themselves first. Otherwise, you cross that thin line and create a life long handicapped dependent. Many will think I'm cold and mean, and when it comes to the survival of this great country, I am. Peace, I rest my case. There is so much crud and other obsolete stuff built up in the economy that only a rebirth can save the whole thing from collapsing.

But, the sad thing is we don't have a strong nuclear family and moral value system in place to nurture us through a normal rebirth. It is good that we live in a land of luxury and plenty, but it can lull one into a false sense of security. Actually it only takes food, shelter, and warmth to survive. Sure, these three simple things are taken for granted and is seen as a given, but don't kid yourself about their importance. One can't eat a fine car or a million dollars.

It may come a time when a garden and a shotgun are worth more than a million dollars.

In the year of our Lord this twenty sixth day of December two thousand four A.D... From the desk of Freddie L. Sirmans, Sr.
A tender moment
I, Freddie L. Sirmans, Sr. have fought to keep my composure because I think it is weak, unmanly and self serving to succumb to soft and mushy feelings. But, I decided to give in and share a brief glimpse of my tender side.

As a small child I was called a cry baby because I would cry at the drop of a hat. Today as much as I know better, I still feel crying is a weakness and will go to great lengths to conceal it. But, I'm going to let the secret out, which is, I never really stopped being a cry baby. At the age of sixty two I still will cry at the drop of a hat. Recently in my home town I sat in my vehicle waiting for what seemed like an endless stream of motor cycles to pass. Strapped to the bikes with bungee cords were toys.

There were choppers, hogs, sidecars, and bikes of every make and model. The riders were black, white, red, brown, yellow, bearded, clean shaven, muscular, tall, short, fat, slim, young, old, male, and female. But, they all had one thing in common, a toy to light up the face of a needy child with a smile for Christmas. As I sat there alone in my vehicle, teary eyed, I had to repeat three words, "Thank you God" over and over to keep from being over flooded.

I could not help but think of the Frenchman (Alexis de Tocqueville) that came in search to understand the secret of America's greatness. After some time he came to a conclusion. "America is great because America is good." Indeed, I do concur. Amen. PS: (Later, I've learned De Tocqueville Didn't actually say those words, but to me it doesn't matter, it's still the truth.)

In the year of our Lord this sixth day of January two thousand five A.D.
From the desk of Freddie L. Sirmans, Sr.

I've changed.

I truly believe that the Lord work in mysterious ways. Also, I believe we all have a guarding angel, but most of us don't listen. To arrive at my present stage in life I know I did not make it without some unexplained help. A few time in my past, suddenly out of nowhere I just knew not to do something that later I found would have done me great harm. During my early years I was not as responsible or committed as I should have been.

Harsh physical discipline as a child kept me in line. But, it left me overly passive, insecure, and neurotic. The down side to being neurotic is it makes one super aware of their actions and surroundings. Then anything forbidden or threatening in anyway can become an over powering distraction, which can rob one of peace of mind when around others. The only truly way out is to learn to forgive and do good. As a child, below the surface at my core there was no real commitment or conviction for hardly anything.

There were very little I wouldn't do if I thought I could get away with it and no one would ever know. I've come a long ways. I've changed. To the best of my judgment I'm going to forgive and do good in this world for the rest of my life. "So many mentally toils and snares I've overcome and am still standing with a positive thankful attitude." So many times if left entirely up to me it would have been easy to just end it all, but it's not an option to intentionally hurt my family or loved ones.

For some reason an individual once told me, "We are affected by your struggle, why you don't just end it all," my response was mute, but I felt no-way hosa. Indeed, the price for super great wisdom doesn't come without great suffering. Thank you God. Thank you God. Thank you God.....

A fact is we all too some degree would like something for nothing, but wise men know it is a fantasy and there is no such thing. Anybody that has read some of my writing knows that I sometimes refer to laws of nature. I fairly often refer to the law of "Natural selection." There is another natural law of nature that the liberals have exploited to the utmost ever since the new deal.

Through this law they have gained enough power now to take civilization back to the Stone Age. Because of this law if you feed a mangy dog or any other animal one time he will show up day after day for a very long time. It is why sales and bargains works. It is why some people rob and steel. It is why it is so hard to get most kids to hit the books and study hard. It is why the liberals have been able to grow this sugar daddy welfare state to the brink of taking civilization back to the Stone Age.

The law I'm referring to is "The course of least resistance." Just about everything in nature is influenced by this law, even electricity. From lack of wisdom we have allowed the welfare state to take us down the road of least resistance ever since the new deal. While we were going down the course of least resistance road the fabric that holds every society together were rotting away until now we have almost no means of surviving an economical collapse.

The nuclear family has been the foundation of every society knows to man since the dawn of history. Now, the welfare state has destroyed nearly seventy percent of the African American nuclear family system. Our morals and values are what come out of Hollywood. And as for bartering capacity we have practically none. We depend mostly on huge centralized farms and animal factory farms for our food which may be hundreds of miles away.

In a mass national disaster the grocery shelves will be clean within hours and within days hungry people may create bottle necks everywhere. Respect for someone else's property will be something foreign. Folks, I may be letting my imagination run away, but I hope you get the point, that there is no substitute for good morals and values. I'm a writer and sometimes my imagination is just that my imagination.

Seriously, I do believe it will take a miracle to save this great nation. However, I do believe in miracles. Praise the Lord.

IS BIG ECONOMY PACKAGE A PIPE DREAM?

I believe the core problem that is destroying the United States economy is the ever raising "High cost of living and dwindling buying power of the dollar." That said, I don't see this big economy package eliminating the high cost of living or the dwindling buying power of the dollar in any meaningful way, I see just a finger in the dike. What I see is going to speed up the higher cost of living and the dwindling buying power of the dollar.

The result of huge increases in government spending and countless new hidden taxes is going to push the cost of living even further out of reach. The high cost of living is already eating us alive and the only thing that's going stop it or slow it down is lower taxes and less government spending, there is no other way out. The fact is western civilization is not going to survive holding on to their welfare states, the cost is simply going to bleed the United States and Western Europe to death.

The United States needs to decide which more important, survival is or to keep feeding the welfare state beast. So far it seems we have decided to keep feeding the welfare state beast. Time is running out, we can no longer afford the cost of the welfare state. When not enough people can keep up with the "Cost of living" they can't buy new cars or much of anything else. If you think that is bad, remember the economy is only one leg of the four legged survival stool.

The economy leg is the last leg holding us up. The nuclear family leg, the culture leg, and the bartering capacity leg for all practical purpose have already failed due to the welfare state. Never forget, the future is never set in stone, man always has the free choice by his actions to chart his own destiny. Long live the great United States of America. Never, count America out.

Why do you think a poor uneducated neurotic South Georgia, USA country boy like me can break through all of the negative childhood myths and ignorance and one day sound the alarm for America's survival? The abilities of freedom and a free people are omnipotent.

I, Freddie L. Sirmans, Sr. repeat, there ain't gonna be a "Great depression" in the United States of America, It ain't gonna happen. Our welfare state has closed off that sad option.

We are going to face something much, much worse. I've been screaming and hollering in the wiliness for many years now about the dangers of a welfare state and no one would listen and still won't listen.

If the economy collapses we are going to zip right past that stage to the next stage, total chaos. Here is my reasoning on this, we have no emergency bartering capacity backup (food wise) to survive on and buy time to reorganize.

Our nuclear family system is almost in ruins, which has been the foundation for human survival since the dawn of history. And lastly our moral and family values has been reduced to "What feels good do it." To sum it up, we have no societal infrastructure left to sustain us through a great depression. I can only hope and pray that my observation is wrong. Society survived on trade and bartering long before money was invented.

Bartering is the base and foundation of any economic system and should never be completely destroyed. In a true free market place economy there will always be underground bartering. Then along comes this winner takes all welfare state beast that takes away the need for the nuclear family, the culture and moral shield, and the backup bartering capacity of small farmers and home gardeners.

Folks, when you destroy your bartering economical base and foundation you have nothing to return home to, you are left lost in an economical no man land. However, we do have one last fighting chance of economical survival left, but that mean starving the welfare state beast. Folks, I hate saying it but history has proven that power concedes nothing; we are locked in on a course leading to total collapse.

Big brother will never concede one inch of their power back to the people. Nothing short of a divine miracle will break this welfare state beast's tax bite on the throat of the United States economy.

WILL THE EURO TRUMP THE DOLLAR

The good Sumerian liberal politicians that have the people's best interest at heart decided a few years back to reward the old folks by taxing their social security checks. Yet, there was no outrage, and the old folks still keep voting the same liberal politicians back in office, why is this? I'll tell you why. When someone has bought into the big lie that there is something for nothing in life they can be film flamed.

Right now many of the same politicians that have sold this country down the river is still running their pie in the sky something for nothing shell game successful when they know the cupboard is bare. No outside enemy is here taking our rights and country away, we are willingly voting into office smooth talking flamboyant people with the gift of gab, and expecting them and the government to take care off us, how sad. This country is broke, and we sure can't eat promises.

I'm repeating myself again, no one can understand the basics of how an economy works unless he starts with bartering. You can talk about the stock market, interest rates, compound interests, government bonds, municipal bonds, derivatives, Commodities, pork bellies, or whatever, but if you don't understand the need for a bartering capacity foundation, you are lost in terms of long time survival.

This sugar daddy hand out welfare state has shut down the underground bartering capacity backup that have existed throughout the history of civilization. This welfare state is winner take all and leaves nothing, except starvation and back to the Stone Age. I'm no fan of Russia, but with the breakup of the former Soviet Union at least they had some bartering capacity in place. Their bartering capacity was the only thing that kept them afloat.

Sure, the US economy is the most powerful economy in the world but our welfare state economy have killed off almost all capacity to barter to survive in time of distress. It is never wise to have all of your survival eggs in just one basket. The saddest thing about this whole situation is the liberals has this nation by the throat, and will never let up until all individual responsibility and accountability is choked off.

Within their shallow minds, they care and want to do good, but in reality their eyes have never been pried open by true hardship to survive. Anyone that thinks that great character can be built without struggle has never been severely tested. Because when the chips are down and your friends walk away, how many will be able to ignore the taste of bitterness and never look back, certainly not one that thinks the world owes him a living.

There is no such thing as something for nothing. The US has had its nearly eighty year's grace period of free spending, now its pay the piper time or mother nature is going to take it out of our hide, it may mean, even back to the stone age. Enough said, let's move on.

I see where more and more people are beginning to flee the dollar and run to the Euro for financial security. It may be a case of jumping out of hot water into the fire. Like the dollar the Euro does not have a gold backup and in my view is not nearly as strong as even a weaken dollar. What surprises and baffles me is why so many even learned economists are so ignorant of the very basics of economical survival.

What are they teaching in economic school, many do not have a clue as to the bartering foundation? Their priority is all wrong. Sure, money is extremely important, but it is not the most important thing to survive, people survived long before money was invented. Many primitive societies even to this day survive without money.

The priority follows in this order; food, shelter, warmth, culture, bartering, and then currency (money). Money only allows a society to survive more efficiently. Even culture in the long run is more important than money. Without a culture with a strong nuclear family system and a strong moral code in place money will not matter because there will not be any unity to hold the society together.

I believe civilization would not be where it is today without the Christian religion and its moral code. The main reason I believe the Christian religion has allowed so much advancement is its emphasis on love and forgiveness. It may seem like a small thing that does not really matter, but without it, a society tends to stay primitive.

Just look around, there are countries that without outside trade and influence definitely would regress back to the primitive stage, especially culture-wise. Following bartering a currency is next in line of priority, but that means a currency that have it value in itself or a guaranteed backup.

There must be a physical accountability currency to protect a society's culture because as human being we are controlled by our greed and self-interest. Also, a physical accountability currency would have purged out all of the liberal anti-survival threats we face today, such as men marrying men, women marring women, illegal aliens with driving licenses, and on and on.

There has never been a society that changed course even knowing it is headed toward total disaster, because greed and self-interest coupled with power concedes nothing. Right now with the financial condition this country is in the liberal and even conservative politicians will never voluntarily stop reckless spending without a physical barrier stopping them.

It is the nature of man to push the envelope or go the limit unless physical stopped, a real currency does that. The stock market, interest rates, and compound interest are all side issues; it is like playing the game monopoly in real life unless there is a gold backup. It just takes around five generations to catch up with us.

If a country does not have any fall back underground bartering capacity and a physical accountability currency, it is truly living in a fantasy world. There has never been and never will be a government that will not go broke at some point. To all of those running to the Euro, just remember that civilization was built on a physical accountability currency, not wealth based only on trust and faith.

A Lack of a gold backup and the welfare state have destroyed our small farmers and home gardeners, our underground bartering capacity backup, and our once strong nuclear family system. Now, same sex marriages and other anti-survival forces have the power to bring down the whole system.

The million-dollar question is: Can western civilization survive? Sad to say, I have my doubts. Something will come about, but it may not be freedom.

You can have all of the money in the world, but if it won't buy you food you can't survive, you can't eat money. Money is not going to do you any good if everyone is using their own fuel to stay warm and is unwilling to sell you any. Money is not going to do you any good if there is no strong culture and good morals because everyone is going to be at each others throat with no peace without force.

That is why individual freedom as we have known so long is on its way out, unless our welfare state is dismantled. Only power and forced authority will keep order when individual responsibility and accountability have been destroyed throughout western civilization by the welfare states.

The only thing that has a fighting chance of saving individual freedom and western civilization is to dismantling or privatizing out of the welfare state. There is no other way, but the politicians in office will never give up one inch of their provider role power.

The welfare state politicians are the ones that have given tax break incentives to businesses to move off shore and sell cheap labor goods back into the US with no penalty. When all is said and done it is the welfare state politicians that have sold the US down the river not the corporations.

EVery business's goal is to survive and make as much profit as possible that is just doing what a business does. Corporations has no authority or power to force it's will on anyone, or do anything, except with the permission and approval of the welfare state.

A person always has the option to quit and find another job. All of this blame big business and the corporations is just sheer ignorance.

It is sheer demagoguery; you hear it every day on the campaign trail, just blame the big bad corporation boogie man, it's sick. The hidden hand in all of this selling off of America has been and still are the liberal politicians of both political parties putting their greed for power above the long term survival of their country. As to the global economy, there is no saving it.

The fact is, a global economy is really a fool's game, because there can never be a completely successful global economy without there first being a global military force to enforce it. Do you think the American people would pay all of these high property taxes, income taxes, school taxes, special purpose taxes, and other taxes without the welfare state enforcing it?

Plus, there are all types of license fees, permit fees, and other mandated fees. There is no way the people would comply without force. It is the same way with a global economy, other countries are never going to pay or play fair without force.

Today no one truly owns a home or anything else in this country with the cost of property taxes. And, you better pay on time or penalties will still take it from you. The foundation of freedom is the ability to own private property. But that can't be if you can't pay the taxes, the welfare state is on its way to owning all of the property.

As to a currency, a currency is supposed to represent spent human energy of some form. When traced back through bartering, spent energy and sweat is supposed to be what created something of value. To just crank up the printing presses and print worthless paper money without a gold backup is the same as those announcing they have invented a perpetual motion engine. It is an illusion. It is impossibility.

Sure, you can get away with running a phony economy like this for eighty to a hundred years but it is going to eventual catch up with you. But, during all of these years it is slowly rotting away the nation's means to survive when hard times come; it is slowly rotting away the nation's culture, it is slowly rotting away the nation's moral fabric, the nation's nuclear family system, and the nations bartering capacity in case the economy fails. It is destroying all of the necessary things that hold a society together. My God! Why can't more people see this?

Lately I hear the term "Protect the Children" and we know what is best for the children. In my view it is like "The three blind men examining an elephant." I can't remember all of the details, but all three came away with a different conclusion, one thought the legs were tree trunks. From a big picture point of view it is impossible for the welfare state to truly protect the children.

Until recently, going back over five thousand years the children were always protected because of one simple fact, the parents needed them for survival. Today most parents see children as love items to be pampered and doted upon. Kids are almost never seen as future meal tickets, which they are. The welfare state has taken away the need for the male head of household and the need to raise children like ones life will depends on it.

The supreme natural law of human survival is based on a survival need, and bleeding heart do good liberals have all but destroyed any need for responsibility, accountability, or anything else. I'm totally against any abuse of any child for any reason, period. God save us.

Lose weight without trying.
Anyone familiar with my writing knows that I have a super strong belief in "positive thinking" to change behavior. To those that don't know what positive thinking is, I will explain. It is a technique to change behavior;

take a phrase or quote and repeats it over and over to yourself. It doesn't need to be repeated aloud.

However, to be effective it must be repeated at least fifty or more times every day. The more times it is repeated the faster it will work because it is the repeating process itself that breaks through to the subconscious. To apply the technique to losing weight one first must decide on a desired goal weight.

An example: If ones desired goal weight is "150LBS," then one must visualize 150LBS when repeating the positive thinking quote. This is a new more powerful quote that I have just developed and is testing it on myself, and decided to share it with you. Hopefully, we all will physical reach our goal weight.

The quote is: "I can keep my weight down to "X LBS." through God which strengthens me." The through God part can be omitted or changed to fit ones own deity. It may take as long as six months to fully kick in, but if one doesn't quit the repeating process is guaranteed to get results. Just keep saying the quote, God will make a way out of no way. Mighty forces will come to your aid. Just keep saying the quote, God will make a way out of no way. Mighty forces will come to your aid.

Health tip bonus:
A heaping tablespoon full of any leafy
vegetable mixed with your meal at least twice
a day will ease almost all digestive problems.

WHAT'S UP WITH THE HOUSING FORECLOSURE SCARE?

Let me, Freddie L. Sirmans, Sr analyze and
dissect the inner working of the US economy.
After the "New deal" the liberals set in
motions this inflationary spiraling economy
we have today. Inflationary spiraling is when
government gives mass amounts of money to
individuals to meet whatever price the
merchants demand, thereby allowing the
merchants to dictate the cost of living.

That is a no-no; the cost of living should be
dictated by the public's ability to pay in the
free market place. That was the beginning of
the inflationary spiraling we have today. The
first thing is the government doesn't have
any money unless it is taken from
somewhere. That is why government should
stay out of the market place as much as
possible and take only enough funds to
defend the country, run the government and
not take on a provider role or any other
burdens.

In a natural non inflationary economy the
merchants can't charge more than the poor
people can afford and stay in business

because of their numbers. There are never enough rich people to support too higher prices. Throughout history when one couldn't afford to pay he turned first to the extended family, the church, community organizations, and lastly the government. The government should never have gone past funding community wise things, such as kitchens and shelters.

Giving money to individuals on an individual basis is the dumbest thing a government can do in a democracy for long term survival. It sets up the system we are in today where the merchants need to raise prices higher and higher to stay in business, and the government needs to raise taxes higher and higher to support it's provider role, so the poor can support the merchants higher and higher prices in a never ending upward spiral.

Many hard working people are as much as ten years behind the curve and are falling farther and farther behind by not getting a raise every year. If you think that is bad, look at the destruction it has done to the nuclear family, our bread basket small farmers, our manufacturing base, our bartering capacity, and on and on. But, here is the real kicker that most American doesn't think about; this whole system depends on mass money circulation to survive, whereas a natural free market system doesn't.

If money circulation slows to a crawl it could collapse the whole system and starve most us to death. Whether true or not, the old "Sling" expressions of liberals booming the economy with mass social spending and conservatives booming the economy by fighting wars may not work anymore. The people are just about taxed out and so much of what we buy is made overseas that the only thing that really booms the economy anymore is mass building construction.

So, if house building and construction slows to a crawl we will be in for a lot of hurt. After restocking and paying operating cost the profit margin for some retail businesses can be as low as three percent. The billions of US dollars going overseas to purchase foreign made products and merchandise are not circulating back here in our economy. Sure, they may buy US treasure bonds and some big ticket items, but that's still not very much circulation to help boost and keep our economy healthy.

That is why I rant and rail so hard about our government lessening its burdens through privatizing. There is no painless way out of the fix our economy is in but at least privatizing is a step toward sanity and long term survival.

May God bless and keep this great free nation always.

Lose weight without trying.

Anyone familiar with my writing knows that I have a super strong belief in "positive thinking" to change behavior. To those that don't know what positive thinking is, I will explain. It is a technique to change behavior; take a phrase or quote and repeats it over and over to yourself. It doesn't need to be repeated aloud.

However, to be effective it must be repeated at least fifty or more times every day. The more times it is repeated the faster it will work because it is the repeating process itself that breaks through to the subconscious. To apply the technique to losing weight one first must decide on a desired goal weight.

An example: If ones desired goal weight is "150LBS," then one must visualize 150LBS when repeating the positive thinking quote. This is a new more powerful quote that I have just developed and is testing it on myself, and decided to share it with you. Hopefully, we all will physical reach our goal weight.

The quote is: "I'm going to keep my weight down to "X LBS." through God which strengthens me." The through God part can be omitted or changed to fit ones own deity. It may take as long as six months to fully kick in, but if one doesn't quit the repeating process is guaranteed to get results. Just keep saying the quote, God will make a way out of no way. Mighty forces will come to your aid.

IS THE USA DAY OF RECKONING UPON US?

A very wise general once said, "Never give an order you know is not going to be obeyed." When I look back and analyze the decline and destruction of western civilization I believe abandoning the gold standard was the time bomb. Nothing else I can think of could have brought down western civilization. With a gold standard there would be no welfare state today. There would be no destruction of the nuclear family.

There would be no inflationary spiraling. There would be no illegal immigration invasion. There would be no complete moral breakdown. The physical boundary of a physical accountability currency would have purged out anti-survival threats long before they could bring down the whole system. You know the economy is completely out of balance when the essential workingman is barely surviving while many nonessential professions are raking in millions upon millions.

The day of reckoning looms on horizon. However, there is never a set prediction for the future; man always has the option through his action to determine his future. "The horse is out of the barn, the tooth paste is out of the tube, the train has left the station, no need to cry over spilled milk, a day late and a dollar short, you can't turn back the clock," or some other metaphor is how I see it.

There is no painless way out of sleeping in the bed we have made. Not even the fall of the Roman Empire could destroy western civilization, but I assure you the welfare states can and will. The only burdens the government should have in a democracy are the responsibility for internal and external protection, and other administrative costs.

Then if the economy collapsed the government should still have enough treasure to survive to regroup. Our government has taken on the burden of supporting the welfare state and if the economy collapses the masses of dependents will be left with no means to survive. Even now, the USA government should be weaning itself of its masses of dependents burden, but is instead headed in the opposite directions and taking on more burdens.

In my view it is insane, shallow, and living in the moment. To me this makes our long term survival a roll of the dice. The only thing that is going to give western civilization a fighting chance is a lean and mean government with proud, independent, and self-sufficient nuclear families, otherwise get prepared to start praying several times a day. And lastly, you can write me off as a kook, so be it, but history will be the final judge.

I'm sure those that believe in one world government see me as irrelevant.

Lose weight without trying.
Anyone familiar with my writing knows that I have a super strong belief in "positive thinking" to change behavior. To those that don't know what positive thinking is, I will explain. It is a technique to change behavior; take a phrase or quote and repeats it over and over to yourself. It doesn't need to be repeated aloud.

However, to be effective it must be repeated at least fifty or more times every day. The more times it is repeated the faster it will work because it is the repeating process itself that breaks through to the subconscious. To apply the technique to losing weight one first must decide on a desired goal weight.

An example: If ones desired goal weight is "150LBS," then one must visualize your body as slim when repeating the positive thinking quote. This is a new more powerful quote that I have just developed and is testing it on myself, and decided to share it with you.

Hopefully, we all will physical reach our goal weight.

The quote is: "I can keep my weight down to "X LBS." through God which strengthens me." The through God part can be omitted or changed to fit ones own deity. It may take as long as a year or longer to fully kick in, but if one doesn't quit the repeating process is guaranteed to get results. Just keep saying the quote, God will make a way out of no way. Mighty forces will come to your aid. "Substitute your goal weight in place of the X."

Health tip bonus:
A heaping tablespoon full of any leafy vegetable mixed with your meal at least twice a day will ease digestive problems.

THE INNER ME!
There are many people that wonder what make Freddie L. Sirmans, Sr. tick? Well, I'm not so sure myself and I know me better than anyone. Personality-wise, I being a writer am almost like a fish out of water. I may not show it but deep down I can be secretive, suspicious minded, and reclusive to a fault. All of that said, I still decided to share some of my inner thoughts and beliefs.

There is one thing I never want and have waged an internal battle and struggle against all of my life that is self-pity. No one can truly know what goes on in the mind of another human being. The self-pity thing! The first neurotic symptom I experienced as a very young child was a physical look of self-pity for being physical punished for wetting the bed. I believe the end product of any adult is mostly what comes out of childhood.

It's not talked about, but the human mind will go to extreme lengths to aid in ones survival, especially the very young. The neurotic self-pity look was my minds way of trying to assure my survival. The mind can give an abused child super natural sexual powers of projection, which may cause all kinds of unintended consequences. Even when one has great genes I believe the environment is still by far the biggest factor in how one turns out.

Whoa! Don't be so quick to judge, the lord works in mysterious ways. I truly think God for the way I am, or what I do have. The hardest thing is to learn to love and forgive something you hate and something's you shouldn't, but things about yourself you should. Self-shame, self-guilt, self-pity, etc. are emotions that can completely disable any human being. Many things that most people take for granted are cut off to me.

Sure, I could spend a lifetime learning to do things now cut off to me, but I feel when destiny reaches out and selects you for a mission it is because of who you are, not who you want to be.

I never set out to be a writer, I just got tired of being mistreated, and felt at least somebody would know Freddie L. Sirmans, Sr. deserves some respect. There has been no stone unturned looking into my life. There! I've said it! I have bared part my soul! How much will it cost me?

STARVING IS THE DEADLIEST THREAT TO THE USA!

Look at history! In any profession when an original thinker like me speaks reality and common sense professional ideologues has always closed their eyes and ears. Look at the closed minds Sister Kenny (nurse) faced in trying to aid polio victims. The buggy whip industry had a closed mind against the automobile. And the automobile industry had a closed mind against leaving any trolley car tracks in place anywhere in the country.

However, reality can be put off only so long, then it will start settling in whether one likes it or not. The rock hard cold reality is, "The galloping cost of living and the dwindling buying power of the dollar" is what's killing our economy. No amount of bail outs or stimulus packages is going to save us because that is barking up the wrong tree.

Anyone reading enough of my writing soon realizes that it must be super natural inspired or the ranting of a lunatic. You decide!

Food is the number one priority for survival. In the end food is going to be the real undoing of this welfare state. None of the other lesser priorities such as culture, bartering, currency (money), or even the lack of oil are the deadliest threats to this nation. The deadliest threat to this nation is a hundred million or more people starving to death when the economy collapses.

And anybody that thinks it can't happen is a Damn fool. We have almost no bartering capacity. And a strong nuclear family system is almost nonexistent. Those are the two primary things that have allowed civilization to exist for over five thousand years.

Our morals and values are so corrupted that when the going gets rough millions of people are going to have to die un-necessarily just to maintain order. The masses of welfare state dependents have no true sense of self-discipline or self-initiative, they think the federal government is omnipotent. The welfare state is what killed off this nation's small farmer and home gardeners, they was this nation's emergency breadbasket.

They furnished this nation with a huge

bartering capacity and would have been the backup to sustain this nation during a financial collapse or nuclear crisis. They got this nation through the great depression. Our current welfare state has left us with almost no bartering capacity or hardly any means of surviving if the government does go belly-up.

A nation with no bartering capacity is like having a dagger aimed at its heart in terms of long term survival. Sure, the huge centralized mechanized factory farms are feeding us now, but provide almost no national bartering capacity. They are extremely dependent on mass quantities of fuel made from oil, and they are hundreds of miles away.

That means if there are bottle necks or fuel problems, millions of mouths could go without food. As it is now this nation could be in grave danger even with a small national crisis that last over three days. People could start hoarding and bottle necks could pop up everywhere. Yet, I'm seen as a nut case for wanting to be prepared to survival under all conditions.

Big liberal media knows who I am, because I've been out here beating the bushes for a lot of years, now (no pun intended). The good thing about beating the bushes is, if nothing else, it eventually drives the political snakes out into the open.

With modern political polling almost every politician is just pandering to what he thinks the people want to hear. So, a word of warning is careful what you wish for, you just might get it, but in sheep clothing. I have personally seen opportunist people change from like night to day with just a small taste of money or power.

Freddie L. Sirmans' lecture on understanding an economy.

The fact is very few people today actually understand how an economy is supposed to works, even some learned economist. The minute the government took on a free cash give-out provider role the US destruction die was cast. Under current conditions it is now impossible to control inflation. I feel it necessary to give a brief lecture in my opinion on how an economy works.

John produces enough food for his family and him to eat plus a little extra to sell for a profit. But John can only produce a small amount for profit. So, to make more profit John needs a helper, but he must share the extra profit with the helper in the form of a salary. He is now a proprietor and can continue to expand as long as his profit margin will allow it. The keyword is profit, profit, profit, and more profit.

To all of these liberals that think jobs just drop out of heaven and big business is the boogie man, try living without profit. An economy actually consists of only two players no matter how advanced and complicated it becomes, a seller and a buyer. Anyone else involved is just crashing the party. Let's use merchant as the seller and consumer as the buyer.

This evil boogie man that's called "Inflation" can never take over a true natural economy. That is because the merchants can never charge more than the poorer consumers can afford and stay in business. From necessity a third player must enters the economy picture for security reasons, that player is the government.

Government itself is not part of a functional economy. It is a necessary parasite that is needed to protect the economy and society. Government is not a threat to an economy as long as it takes its cut off the top and fulfills its role as a protector. The trouble starts when government takes its tax revenue cut and starts interfering in the economical process itself thereby disrupting the natural balance between the merchant and the consumer.

There are only two players, the merchant and the consumer in an economy. So, when government uses its take to subsidize the poorer group of consumers on an individual basis, it allows the merchants to survive their price raise for everyone and ignite inflation on everyone.

The balance arm is a strong nuclear family. Throughout history before the welfare state a merchant could never raise prices above what the poor could afford to pay because the poor could turn to the nuclear family for support. Plus, there were many small farmers and home gardeners and never enough rich and well-to-do to support the merchant's too high prices.

There must be a government to protect a society from internal and external threats. The thing about government is it has the power and the guns. So, dictator and authoritarian type governments take over and runs the whole show. Nothing has changed, authoritarian type governments have never been able feed themselves.

Throughout distance history they would conquer other countries and make them slaves or work almost for nothing. Only free people with a free market place will produce enough for everyone to eat. Otherwise, one will do just enough to keep from getting shot.

There is no problem or threat to an economy with government in the picture. And having government in the picture will not activate inflation if it avoids handing out money on an individual basis. Government spending itself doesn't activate inflation; it's how it does the spending.

Government can spend like crazy and build hospitals, bridges, roads, or whatever and it won't activate inflation because that doesn't affect the relationship between the merchants and the consumers. The government can give the poor food, clothing, housing or whatever and it still won't activate inflation. But, the one thing the government should never do because it will wake up and unleash the sleeping monster called "Inflation."

That one thing is the government giving out free cash money to the poor or anyone else on an individual basis. The "Individual basis" is the deadly time bomb fuse. What that does is disrupt the natural selection process between the merchant and the consumer and activates a never ending inflationary spiraling monster. How this work is there are never enough rich people to keep overly high cost merchants in business.

So, the government with good intentions gives the poor enough free cash money to afford the merchant's high price. In the beginning that made all parties happy. Then the government raised taxes to give out more cash so the poor could support even higher merchant prices, and upped the ante even higher by throwing in food stamps and countless social programs.

The merchants called, and again raised their prices. And again the government called, then raised taxes even higher, and around and around it goes in this never ending inflationary spiral. That is what got us to where we are today.

Trading and bartering have been around as long as civilization itself. A true free market place will always produce enough food to feed everyone at an affordable price if allowed to. All that is necessary is for the government to get the hell out of the way, and stick to its true role as administrator and protector of society. That means collect the taxes its due, and the economy will take care of its self with government out of the way.

It won't be pretty but if allowed to the natural selection process and entrepreneurs will feed the poor and everyone at an affordable price. However, that will never take place when dictators and over controlling governments choke off self-initiative, self-greed, and self-interest. The above are the most powerful energy packed motivating forces in our human makeup. Sure, you must control these forces but never completely choke them off if you want a rich and powerful society.

Some may ask, what about all of these

people depending on the government. In my view the government caused the problem and is responsible for providing whatever is necessary for these people to survive. But, we must get off this ever increasing merry-go-round inflationary spiral before inflation eats up the last crumb of any dollar buying power.

Almost everyone thinks without government help the poor can't make it, but in reality it was just the opposite before the welfare state destroyed everything. There are over five thousand years of history that backs me up on this. Sure, the poor will always need help from somewhere, but it should come from the nuclear family, the extended family, the church, and community organizations.

Human survival is based on need involving a natural selection process. When the government with its power becomes a sugar daddy provider it takes away the survival need for the strong nuclear family, extended family, etc. Now, if the economy collapses the government can't provide for its dependents and other debts and burdens, and all I can say is "Lord helps us."

Even the people that remember the "The Hoover days" with the struggles during the "Great depression" never had their spirits dampened like they are today. I will not break my pen, I will never stop trying to sound the alarm as long as there is breath in me, and this welfare state is slowly skinning this nation alive. I want my grand children to be free.

In my view when it comes to forms of government, nothing is more deadly for destruction than a welfare state, not even communism or socialism. The welfare state is a new monster that only came about within the last fifty years since money no longer has value in itself or a gold backup.

The reason why I view the welfare state so deadly is in its deception, it lulls almost everyone to sleep until it is too late. In its early and middle stage almost everyone is fat and happy while it slowly eats away and destroys the nuclear family foundation and the very things that allow a society to survive. And In the final stage nothing can stop its inflationary spiraling from spinning out of control.

The billion dollar question is what is the wisest course to take out of this dilemma? This is my opinion and advice: The first priority is to save the federal government at all cost. To me that mean the government must slowly start jettisoning its social provider role and all other financial burdens through privatization, except the bare necessities.

It should slowly start privatizing out of all nonessential government burdens except the department of defense, treasure, interior, and one or two others. And above all, lower taxes not higher taxes are the only way out. To me that is the wisest course to take if this country is to have a fighting chance to survive. Sure, you can call me insane, a fool, a nut case or whatever, but that is my opinion and advice. No one is forced to believe me.

There really is no choice, because Mother Nature is cocked and ready to enforce its own law of "The survival of the strongest and the fittest" any day now. You can take my exceptional great wisdom with a grain of salt, or you can take it to the bank, It is out of my hand, I've did my duty.

The founding fathers knew what an all powerful government would do; they had seen it in old Europe. With the constitution they did all they could to enact laws to keep out of the driver's seat a government of unlimited power. Fast forward to today. The tenth amendment is totally ignored.

And I for one don't believe the constitution ever allowed for this almost unlimited taxing power the welfare state has today. It's over folks, the welfare state now has unlimited taxing power to support its super provider role. All we can do is pray and hope for the best.

After hearing a heated discussion on the radio involving the word "Hope" I decided to throw in my two cents. Beliefs like faith, hope, desire, etc. standing alone is practically useless. Anyone living only on faith or hope will die fasting.

However, the key or secret is to add another entirely different ingredient to the mix, that ingredient is "action." Then there is no greater force or power on earth than faith, hope, and courage in action. That is why we had better hurry up and get our act together or it won't be us that inherit the earth, we and all of western civilization may be on our knees praying several times a day.

On another subject, my experience is never let anyone make you an extreme perfectionist. It dehumanizes you. Race baiters and those that will never accept you will find something, if it's not this, it will be that. But, they can never mentally destroy you unless you hate them back. In the end, genuine good and decent people will accept you for who you are and what you are.

Sometimes until a storm passes over, repeating to yourself "May God bless him/her," and mean it, is the Christian thing to do. Fault finders will never stop finding flaws and caring and forgiving people will never stop loving. Balance is the key to life, and never an extreme.

Conservatives almost always win on reduced taxes, a strong defense, and strong family value issues. Otherwise, getting sidetracked and entering the emotionalism arena is like entering the brier patch home of liberals. There all odds are stacked against reason, accountability, and responsibility.

Trying to out liberal liberals has already severely distorted what conservatives truly stand for. If conservatives keep talking about extreme tax cuts like eliminating all taxes on social security, gasoline, farming equipment, diesel fuel, etc. it will scare the hell out of liberals and get voters attention.

I keep reading this sick joke some dear soul is spreading about neurotics. Well, the biggest problem a neurotic has is a super awareness that he/she can't turn off. And that is no fantasy. Myself, I'm a neurotic survival and am thankful that I'm alive and still have my sanity.

Lately I hear the term "Protect the Children" and we know what is best for the children. In my view it is like "The three blind men examining an elephant." I can't remember all of the details, but all three came away with a different conclusion, one thought the legs were tree trunks. From a big picture point of view it is impossible for the welfare state to truly protect the children.

Until recently, going back over five thousand years the children were always protected because of one simple fact, the parents needed them for survival. Today most parents see children as love items to be pampered and doted upon. Kids are almost never seen as future meal tickets, which they are. The welfare state has taken away the need for the male head of household and the need to raise children like ones life will depends on it.

The supreme natural law of human survival is based on a survival need, and bleeding heart do good liberals have all but destroyed any need for responsibility, accountability, or anything else. I'm totally against any abuse of any child for any reason, period. God save us.

Lose weight without trying.
Anyone familiar with my writing knows that I have a super strong belief in "positive thinking" to change behavior. To those that

don't know what positive thinking is, I will explain. It is a technique to change behavior; take a phrase or quote and repeats it over and over to yourself. It doesn't need to be repeated aloud.

However, to be effective it must be repeated at least fifty or more times every day. The more times it is repeated the faster it will work because it is the repeating process itself that breaks through to the subconscious. To apply the technique to losing weight one first must decide on a desired goal weight.

An example: If ones desired goal weight is "150LBS," then one must visualize a slim 150LBS when repeating the positive thinking quote. This is a new more powerful quote that I have just developed and is testing it on myself, and decided to share it with you. Hopefully, we all will physical reach our goal weight.

The quote is: "I can keep my weight down to "X LBS." through God which strengthens me." The through God part can be omitted or changed to fit ones own deity. It may take as long as six months to fully kick in, but if one doesn't quit the repeating process is guaranteed to get results. Just keep saying the quote, God will make a way out of no way. Mighty forces will come to your aid.

WHY THERE IS OUT OF CONTROL VIOLENCE IN THE AFRICAN AMERICAN COMMUNITY?

FREDDIE L. SIRMANS, SR'S LOG: 23 AUGUST 2009, 2051 HOURS.
World wide the welfare state system is on the brink of destroying western civilization. It destroys a nation's culture, its morals, its family values, and any capacity to barter. But, nothing has been more devastated by the welfare state than the African American community in the USA.

The African American people in America have come a long ways. The African American people survived slavery, racism, and unbelievable odds to now have a biracial black man in the white house. A great deal of the credit must go to all Americans because only in America could this happen.

America is still the greatest and all Americans have so much to be proud of. I write what I think and feel and pull very few punches. I'm old enough and remember when I went to an all black high school and violence on campus was something almost unheard of.

I remember as a teenager when there were teen clubs and soda shops where teens could dance and hang out all over town. Now, there are none because there is too much drug use and violence. I remember when teens had almost complete respect for authority.

Now, a five year old will cuss you out. So, what changed? What happen? What went wrong? I'll tell you, the "New Deal and the welfare state" seized the family provider role for itself, that's what went wrong. It seized the provider role and refused to enforce responsibility and accountability in raising the young that came with it.

Once the black man was kicked out of the house there was no one to instill "Self-restraint" in young black males. Those two words "Self-restraint" and the lack of it is why there is so much violence in the African American community. And the welfare state is what destroyed the black nuclear family and community.

All of the young gang banger and others that are committing so much senseless violence has never been conditioned to exercise self-restraint. Consequences in most cases are the furthest thing from a thugs mind. They have never been conditioned to expect swift and sure punishment for wrong doing.

As human we all at times get angry and frustrated, but someone with self-restraint don't just fly of the handle. Someone that has been taught self-restraint as a child is highly unlikely to just strike out with senseless violence.

Sure, almost every human being is capable of committing a violent act if provoked enough, but that is not the case with young black males. They are killing each other at the drop of a hat at an alarming rate all over the country.

The culture mentality must be shaped very young then eighteen years later you will have a productive responsible human being; otherwise you will keep producing die hard gang bangers with a destructive mentality. I think one of the biggest problems in the black community is we don't know who our friends are.

In the end no one is going to save the black community except itself. However, it is about control, who exercises control. Anybody getting fed up and wanting to get tough and throw all of drug dealers and bad guys out is going to run up against the system.

This is America we are ruled by law, but that don't mean a community has to roll over and give up. Good and decent people always have the advantage, because at heart all people want to be thought of as good and decent. That is why culture is the most important thing of all for survival.

I don't care if you can't find but one or two decent people in a whole community those two should bond and shun all corruption. That is how decent people get and exercise control in their community, the wheat must be separated from the chaff meaning the good must be separated from the bad or one apple will spoil the whole barrel.

And there should be no exceptions unless one meets the minimum standards. To me it is the dumbest and silliest thing when supposedly intelligent African Americans wonder why taxicabs don't want to stop for blacks and why many people distrust young black males.

Hell, black taxicab drivers don't want to pick up black males, grow up and take responsibility, and I'm going to keep loving all people No matter who hates or disagrees with me. A community must separate itself from the rotten or the whole batch will be tainted in some way that is not just me saying it, that is reality.

All it takes is for decent people to set a standard, bond, and help and support each other, and hang tough. The corrupted must be shunned with no exception, which is not easy to do because everyone no matter how unfit is somebody's son, daughter, brother, sister, mom, dad, aunt, uncle, grandmother, grand dad, etc.

If a high standard is maintained everyone will

soon want what you have. But, the system will chew you up and spit you out if there is ever a hint of violence to keep anyone out. The bad guys don't give a damn about obeying any law.

You can't beat them at their game, and they can't beat you at yours if you shun them stick together and stay the course. God save our African American community.

PS: Folks, like I keep repeating, its culture, culture, culture, and more culture, meaning a lack of it. There is no denying the fact proportional wise there is more African Americans babies being killed in the womb than anywhere in the world, Lord help us.

WHY DO AFRICAN AMERICANS VOTE OVER 90 PERCENT FOR ONE POLITICAL PARTY EVERY TIME?

I think there is a phenomenon in the human psyche that I'm going to name "The master authority syndrome." I describe it as an awareness of who we perceive to be the master authority in our life. I believe it is something in our human makeup that aids our social survival. I believe nature programmed us to be aware of who is the master authority and to know ones place in the pecking order.

That is my theses, it is not based on any research or anything else, it's just my wisdom and observation. Now, let's apply it to the African American experience in America. African Americans were brought to America as slaves and stripped bare of their language and culture. Back in slavery from the beginning of the new African American psyche, it was drummed in that the white master authority was the only authority.

From a survival point of view African Americans had to keep aware of the white color of the master authority or be perceived as a threat. So, if a black face is mentally blocked from becoming an authority that locked blacks into a permanent dependent role. And one of the pitfalls of being a dependent is sibling rivalry for the approval of the master authority.

Overall the African Americans psyche and mentality has changed very little since slavery. The African American hue ranges from ebony black to almost Lilly white, but overall we still have a white identity mentality. Subconsciously African Americans still perceive black to be dependent and inferior to the preferred white master authority.

As a race today; we still subconsciously see our black brothers as competitors and the enemy in winning white master authority approval. We won't as a race help or support each other in business if there is a choice. Before the welfare state African Americans were slowly shedding their slavery baggage. Back then an all black neighborhood was the safest place a black person could be, but now it is the most dangerous place a black can be.

Back then blacks were very proud of their neighborhoods, some of the houses were run down but everyone took good care of what they had. Black business men were proud to locate in the black neighborhoods. Now, fast forward to today's African American mentality. If we didn't have a black identity bias why would our educated and elites want to get as far away as they can afford from an all black neighborhood.

Many will say the all black neighborhoods are too crime ridden, that may be true, but, blacks were fleeing well before rampant crime took over, the movie "A raising in the sun" proved that. Every other race will establish upper and middle class zones in and around their own community, why not African Americans? Sure, I may criticize African American rich and elites for deserting the black community, but the real true culprit that have destroyed our community pride and racial self-respect is the welfare state. Enough said, I think you get the point.

I know some may think I'm some kind of

black separatist or anti-white hater, but nothing could be further from the truth. In fact I love white people and all people. I don't think Richard M. Nixon was far off the mark with some of the things he said about Africa. African Americans can learn to help and support each other and overcome this vicious sibling rivalry that is killing off so many of our young blacks.

The young African Americans don't know it, but subconsciously they are calling each other nigger and degrading an imaginary black faced rival and enemy that is inferior and doesn't deserve respect. Even though their face is the same color their own desired self image are white. The way out is to learn to love and respect all people. And here is a good formula, just repeat this quote until you learn it by heart. "I can wish all people goodwill no matter how they treat me."

One will never denigrate his immediate family unless he doesn't feel a part of it. It is the same with ones own race family. One will not denigrate his race by using the hated "N" word unless he mentally doesn't feel part of something dear to him. That is because he doesn't mentally know who he is. But, of course there are a few who are ignorant and just don't give a damn. Also, I don't buy this loony idea that "you take the sting out of a degrading word by excess usage."

For African Americans to help and support each other the surest way would be to have a genuine survival need for each other, but that can't happen as long as we have this handout welfare state. "What the hell needs can a poor black man fill for a woman except stud service and companionship at her whim, when uncle sugar with his food stamps and countless social programs is her real provider and caretaker?"

To prove just how far this society has sunk, ninety five percent of the people in this country will think what I just said was sexist and insane. Only about five percent of the people left in this country will have the wisdom to know that what I just said is defending the nuclear family in the face of government abuse by liberal bleeding heart do-gooders.

Without the strong traditional nuclear family this country can't survive a nuclear blast, an economical collapse, or hardly anything. I double dog dare you! Prove me wrong! We have no bartering capacity left or food supplies on hand over a few days. And attacking me personally will prove nothing.

Unless this welfare state is dismantled and the nuclear family restored along with small farmers and home gardeners, this country and western civilization is doomed. What's going to happen when the dollar becomes worthless? Which won't be very much longer? You know something is terrible, terrible wrong when the rats are already secretly leaving the ship. All of these so called experts, especially women you see on TV with the gift of gab talking only rhetoric, they don't have a clue as to what it will take for this great nation to survive under distress.

In my view the freedom we now enjoy may be down to one decade left. I wouldn't be one bit surprised if within ten years the US will be ruled by some kind of civilian junta, following martial law. There is no doubt in my mind that it is only a matter of time before this big spending welfare state economy collapses. The president and congress should be trying to prepare and save the central government by jettisoning as many of its burdens' as possible. But, instead they are adding more and more big government program burdens.

They should be weaning people off the dole to prepare them to survive on their own as much as possible without government. Believe it or not a survival need is what holds a society together. The reason the nuclear family is not supreme anymore is because big government spending took away the survival need for it.

Sure, if government start weaning people there are going to be a lot of hot air and real suffering and even deaths, but the good will far out weigh the bad by bringing back the strong nuclear family savior. That is the only way the US is going to be able to survive a nuclear attack or a collapsed economy, otherwise we can kiss this country goodbye.

When all is said and done, a civilization's survival depends on its offspring. The only true guarantee of a nation's survival is its parents raising responsible children to care for the parents when they are too old to care for themselves. There is no getting around this fact, unless you are one of the few very rich. The nuclear family is the only system know to man that can carry out this feat and guarantee lasting survival.

.

It seems the only time the people in this country are going to wake up is when the checks they receive will hardly buy a loaf of bread. Them all hell is going to break loose, there will be bottle necks everywhere, there will be rioting in the streets everywhere, and there will be starving and mass killings everywhere. And the masses of hungry undisciplined government dependents are going to feel what's yours is now theirs. The freedoms we now enjoy will be down the tube probably forever. As for me, I just hope I'm wrong on my predictions.

.

Mean while back to the subject, the only other way African Americans can help and support each other is through individual "Positive thinking." Just memorize the following quote and repeat it to yourself often, "I can wish all people goodwill no matter how they treat me." The answer to why African Americans vote overwhelming for one party has to do with a dependent mentality.

.

A parent can be a scheming phony, a two faced liar, and even worse, but as long as the kid (African America) is fed and not overly abused the kid is going to support that parent regardless. African Americans somewhere along the line perceived the democrat party as their white master authority parent.

.

It is like the unconditional love a mother has for her child. And the welfare state guarantees that African Americans and the poor stays dependent minded, thereby creating an emotional bond that cannot be broken, until these dependents are forced to grow up, stand on their own and make adult responsible choices.

Lately I hear the term "Protect the Children" and we know what is best for the children. In my view it is like "The three blind men examining an elephant." I can't remember all of the details, but all three came away with a different conclusion, one thought the legs were tree trunks. From a big picture point of view it is impossible for the welfare state to truly protect the children.

.

Until recently, going back over five thousand years the children were always protected because of one simple fact, the parents needed them for survival. Today most parents see children as love items to be pampered and doted upon. Kids are almost never seen as future meal tickets, which they are. The welfare state has taken away the need for the male head of household and the need to raise children like ones life will depends on it.

.

The supreme natural law of human survival is based on a survival need, and bleeding heart do good liberals have all but destroyed any need for responsibility, accountability, or anything else. I'm totally against any abuse of any child for any reason, period. God save us.

.

Lose weight without trying.
Anyone familiar with my writing knows that I have a super strong belief in "positive thinking" to change behavior. To those that don't know what positive thinking is, I will explain. It is a technique to change behavior; take a phrase or quote and repeats it over and over to yourself.

.

It doesn't need to be repeated aloud. However, to be effective it must be repeated at least fifty or more times every day. The more times it is repeated the faster it will work because it is the repeating process itself that breaks through to the subconscious. To apply the technique to losing weight one first must decide on a desired goal weight.

.

An example: If ones desired goal weight is "150LBS," then one must visualize your body as being slim when repeating the positive thinking quote. This is a new more powerful quote that I have just developed and is testing it on myself, and decided to share it with you. Hopefully, we all will physical reach our goal weight. "Substitute your own weight goal in place of the X."

.

The quote is: "I can keep my weight down to "X LBS." through God which strengthens me." The through God part can be omitted or changed to fit ones own deity. It may take as long as a year or longer to fully kick in, but if one doesn't quit the repeating process is guaranteed to get results. Just keep saying the quote, God will make a way out of no way. Mighty forces will come to your aid.

WILLIAM E. B. DU BOIS VERSUS BOOKER T. WASHINGTON.

The old Du bois versus Booker T. Washington two schools of thought still haven't been settled and probably never will. Washington believed that African Americans should take the self reliance route and focus first on learning the basic trade vocations to feed and control their own destiny. He didn't put a priority on integration.

On the other hand, Du bois disagreed openly with Washington and believed that African Americans should not be limited in anyway. Du bois believed that blacks should go the full integration route and focus on the best education possibly. In my view the Du bois way was the right way in theory and it won out on the course blacks should take even to today.

But, as any scientist will tell you what works in theory doesn't necessarily work in practice. In almost all cases for any race to improve overall it must be pulled up from the top because those are the ones with the education and resources to make it happen. For many races there are no color differences, that way they can blend in and move into the mainstream very easily, no problem.

But, for African Americans the norm doesn't work in practice. The two main drawbacks are color difference and African American culture. In my view the biggest failure to uplift African Americans have been the black elite by deserting the black community. Sure, crime and drugs are the excuse now, but that started long before crime and drugs were a big problem; just remember the movie "A raising in the sun."

I understand safety and the need for a pecking order, but blacks could establish middle and upper class zones in or on the edge of black communities if they wanted to. Also, blacks should open businesses and invest back in their own communities like all other races, but it's not happening on a large scale. I think It's something a lot deeper here that African Americans need to face and accept.

I think African Americans as a race are still running away from themselves and their communities. I don't think African Americans as a whole respect themselves unconditional as individuals and as a race with all the flaws and blemishes, unconditionally. I don't think most blacks have a do-for-your-self independent mentality that will make you respect yourself and people that look like you.

I think we as blacks need to face and accept one another with pride and nothing to prove, flawed and scarred but as good as anybody or any race, period. "We don't need a ticket to ride, or to qualify, no one asked to be born, just forgive and accept the past and move on." Do-for-your-self people don't worry about imaginary threats from the past or empty symbolisms; they are too busy working to live a proud independent dignified life.

No one can truly accept and respect you unless you first accept and respect yourself, unconditionally. The color different won't let blacks just blend into the mainstream unnoticed, plus, there is an unspoken negative stereotypical image of blacks as a whole. That unspoken image associates blacks as a whole with property devalue, social baggage, crime, and a few other negative stereotypes.

Still, genes are getting through because in my view big booties are no longer limited to African Americans. The culture drawback is far too many African Americans still unconsciously believe the old black stereotype that black is inferior (that the white man's beer is colder). Far too many blacks still see other blacks as competitors and the enemy in winning mainstream approval.

For that reason we tend not to support one another as a whole in business in the black communities like back in the nineteen forties and fifties.

Lately I hear the term "Protect the Children" and we know what is best for the children. In my view it is like "The three blind men examining an elephant." I can't remember all of the details, but all three came away with a different conclusion, one thought the legs were tree trunks. From a big picture point of view it is impossible for the welfare state to truly protect the children.

Until recently, going back over five thousand years the children were always protected because of one simple fact, the parents needed them for survival. Today most parents see children as love items to be pampered and doted upon. Kids are almost never seen as future meal tickets, which they are. The welfare state has taken away the need for the male head of household and the need to raise children like ones life will depends on it.

The supreme natural law of human survival is based on a survival need, and bleeding heart do good liberals have all but destroyed any need for responsibility, accountability, or anything else. I'm totally against any abuse of any child for any reason, period. God save us.

CAN THE AFRICAN AMERICAN COMMUNITY GET CONTROL OF THE SPREAD OF AIDS?

Well, for what it is worth I decided to add my two cents to the subject, "On the down low." It is no secret that AIDS is far out of proportion in the African American communities and even on Historically Black Colleges and Universities (HBCUs). There must be a reason why this is so. I was the first one that pointed out that the revolving door in and out of the prison system was the leading factor. But, that still doesn't explain why this out of proportion also exists on HBCUs.

That means there must be a culture factor involved. Many believe it is how the African American community defines homosexuality. The general mainstream assumption is that anyone participating in a homosexual act is a homosexual, but that is not what many minority men believe. A great many minority men view homosexuality basically in the same light as masturbation. They view the act in terms of dominant or submission or driver or receiver.

They believe that as long as they are in the dominant role and doing the driving their manhood is not at issue or threatened. They feel they are only acting like a squirrel as long as it is kept secret. Whereas, it is only the one that is in the submissive and receiving role that makes one a homosexual. As a writer I'm not deciding anything, I'm just trying to shine as much light as possible on the true mindset.

To get at the AIDS problem, you first need to

understand what people are really thinking. The fact is, it boils down to the same old saw that is permissive sexual behavior and loose morals. Men have in the past and will always try to get easy sex from whoever will give it up. So, the ultimate AIDS solution lies with the women in this country. They need to stop giving up all of this easy unobligated sex, period.

Back before we had a super big government sugar daddy provider, very few African American women would give up sex without an obligated commitment, and even then he had to be of sound character. Back then If a suitor wouldn't go to church and clean up his act, it was "Her way or the highway," and she had a strong dad or brother that would kick butt to back her up. My solution as always gets the government the hell out of the family provider business.

In my opinion, AIDS in the African American community is approaching the out of control level.

BRIEF BIO OF Freddie L. Sirmans, Sr.
I was born in the early forties in a quiet little Georgia town near the Florida border. It is located at the intersection of U.S. Highway 84 east to west and U.S. Highway 129 north to south. I was delivered by a midwife three days before Christmas, December 22, 1942 in Stockton, Georgia. I was somewhat puny and

was not expected to live. I was the eleventh child in a group that would eventually reach fourteen children.

Unfortunately seven of those fourteen children died before I was born. I was a very sensitive kid, always snotty nosed, but I survived. The old frame house that we lived in was like many houses built around the turn of the century. The kitchen was separated from the living quarters of the main house. In our house, in order to get to the kitchen, you had to go outside and walk down a long porch to reach the kitchen.

We didn't have electric lights, and I remember at night someone older had to carry a kerosene lamp down that seemingly long, long porch, and I would be so afraid. One of my earliest memories in that old house was that I would get a whipping almost every morning for wetting the bed. Also, I remember we had a fireplace, and one morning I was standing with my back to it warming up. I had on some ragged bib overalls. All of a sudden I felt something hot on my leg, and when I looked down, I saw that my pant's leg was on fire.

I took off like a bat out of hell not thinking to smother the fire. I could have easily sustained third degree burns all over my body or lost my life because I would never have stopped running. Fortunately, there was a bed in the room and I ran into it, thereby allowing enough time for my sister Betty and brother Buie to reach me and smother the fire. A large burn mark still covers most of my left leg today. I hated short pants.

It seems as if I was fifteen years old before my mother would let me wear long pants. Most kids my age were wearing long pants, and I felt only little kids wore short pants. I wanted to be mature and grown up, not a little kid in short pants. Most of my earlier years were spent playing and going to the clay hole in the summer. The clay hole was a little man-made lake right beside U.S. Highway 84. Also about one quarter of a mile down the road was New Prospect Baptist Church.

It was at the church where I had to wear short pants and say an Easter speech every Easter. The regular members of the swimming gang were my brothers Buie and Bernard (Rip), my cousin J.E. Burgess, the neighbor kid Spencer Bines, sometimes BoBo Brown, and I. My older brother Marvin was much too mature for us. Our house was the old Corbin home. My grandfather Henry Corbin had moved to Waycross to work for the railroad years ago.

I guess I was around nine or ten when the family left the old Corbin home and moved about four miles to my grandmother's farm. It was the Sirmans' home place that my great-grandfather Steve "Buck", a slave, settled on when he became a free man. My grandmother, Alice Roberts Sirmans, who was born about 15 miles away in Mayday, Georgia, was half Cherokee Indian and half white.

She had been living at the farm when we moved in but moved shortly thereafter to a house in Valdosta, Georgia that my father Charlie and my uncle Freddie had recently built. There on the farm I was expected to do my share of the work. I remember very clearly that complaining did very little good. I remember we had to pick up sweet potatoes after they had been plowed from under the ground.

You had to stay bent over for long periods of time. I would tell my mom or dad that my back was hurting, and they would say, "Boy! What do you mean your back is hurting? You don't even have a back at your age. All you got is gristle." I cropped tobacco and hung it in the barn, but the most hated job was gathering corn in beggar weeds. The corn and the beggar weeds would cause your skin to sting.

Then around 1954 the Sirmans' heirs got together and sold 100 acres of our farm land to Isben Livingston. My dad bought the other 100 acres of the wood land that our house was on which he sold a few years later. In

1955 they closed the two classroom school house in Stockton, Georgia and I attended the seventh grade over in Lakeland, Georgia the county seat. Then in 1956 the Charlie Sirmans' family moved to Valdosta, Georgia.

My dad became a taxi driver. That year I was in the eighth grade, and I started the school year in the old Dasher High School that had been downgraded to a junior high school. At that time a strong disciplinarian, highly moral, and spiritual man, patrolled the halls. That man was Professor J.L. Lomax, the principal, whom the school was later named after. I, like the other students, was terrified and scared to death of being caught in the hall unauthorized.

The new school, Pinedale High, had just been completed. For some reason, I can't remember exactly why, they had added two eighth grade classes to the new high school that first year. Thereafter it was only grades ninth through twelfth. I was in one of the two eighth grade classes attending that first year in 1956. I believe my home room teacher was Ms. Carrie Lissimore.

The principal, Mr. C.C. Hall, the late band director, Mr. C.D Marshall, the chorus and others agreed that the school's new anthem did not rhyme properly with the word Pinedale. Everyone agreed that Pinevale rhymed almost perfectly with the new anthem, so the school was thereafter known as Pinevale High. "Good old Pinevale High we will live and die for you, for you."

I was very insecure and shy in high school and will probably be somewhat shy and insecure all my life. I remember very vividly an incident that happened to me in Ms. Sarah Jones' class. I guess I was in the eleventh or twelfth grade. I had my shoes leaned on their side under my desk, and when I shifted their position on the tile floor it sounded just like someone passing gas. All eyes focused on me, but I never looked up, I just kept my head hung and bowed.

After what seemed like a slow motion minute, Ms. Jones casually and quietly walked over and opened some windows near where I was sitting. After the class was over a small lad that sat right next to me, I can't remember his name, but he walked up and told me, "I know that was your shoe that made that noise" and I told him that it truly was. The reason I mention this incident is that because of my shyness and insecurity at the time I failed to set the record straight.

Even if I didn't have the courage to speak up then, I should have at least went to Ms. Jones later and set the record straight. But instead I remained mute, and to this day as far as I know only that young lad in that whole class knows that I was innocent. Unlike most of today's young men, I was a late bloomer. I had come close, but when I finished high school I had not had a consummated relationship. In fact, my first consummated relationship came around the age of twenty.

In high school I was a jock. I was crazy about girls, but I was afraid to go after them. I excelled in sports, so that became my primary interest. When I graduated in 1961, only two members on the basketball team received scholarships, Oswell Jones and I. We each received basketball scholarships to Fort Valley State. We used to call Oswell the Big "O". To this day I can honestly say Oswell was one of the best basketball shooters I have ever seen.

Even in high school if he got hot he could consistently hit 25 foot jumpers. I am sad to say that he was a victim in a fatal car accident while returning to Atlanta from the "92" Valdosta High School Wildcats State AAAA Championship football game, which Valdosta won. I can still remember one of the chants that the Pinevale High basketball cheerleaders would yell out. "Freddie! Freddie! Freddie! He's is our man, if he can't do it nobody can!"

I finished high school in 1961 and then worked a while at South Georgia Pecan Factory in Valdosta before moving on to

Tallahassee, Florida to attend a little trade school. The name of the trade school was Consolidated Electronics. I went to the school about two hours a day. I managed to get a job in a little bakery and delicatessen shop on Adams Street right around the corner from the old capital building.

I got a room with Mrs. Ford who lived right in front of a funeral home in French Town on Carolina Street. I stayed in Tallahassee for six months until the little trade school ended. After I returned to Valdosta in late 1962, I decided to enlist in the U.S. Air Force. Like most new recruits in basic training, I visited the Alamo in San Antonio. From there I spent two years in Omaha, Nebraska. At that time, GI's didn't make as much money as they do today, but we knew how to party on what we had.

They had a barbecue shack at that time on North 24th Street. They sold a whole slab of rib for about $4.95. Today it would cost a lot more. We would buy a fifth or two of white port or red port wine for about $2.00 a fifth, get fired up, then each of us would get a slab of rib and party into the wee hours. But the downside on duty the next morning I would feel like I had been shot at and missed but S... at and hit. About five months before I left Omaha, I met Janet. That is all I care to say, but she was special and I will never forget her.

I was young and not very responsible in that department. Even when young I tended to talk as a philosopher when someone would listen, and that she certainly would do. I would try to figure out her problems and the why of things. When I left I gave her my home phone number in Valdosta. When she called me while I was on leave, I acted like I didn't want to talk to her. That was the last I ever heard of her. I don't know why, but maybe something in my childhood caused me to feel ill at ease talking to the opposite sex in the presence of my parents.

That is what happened to me when Janet called. When she called I guess I seemed like a different person, like I didn't care. But I really did care. Even today it saddens me how it ended. When I got out on my own and got married that type of behavior didn't occur any more. My last two years in the military were spent in Puerto Rico. I bought a 1952 Studebaker and enjoyed the Caribbean and tropical climate.

I also enjoyed some red beans and rice, the islands' staple, plus some fresh roasted pig. The little coastal town of Aquadilla is where we did most of our partying. The Air Force no longer has a base in Puerto Rico, but at that time in Aquadilla there was a night club called "The Black Stallion" where most of the airmen hung out. I clearly remember one famous patron. She was as black as the ace of spades, and they called her Casa Boo Boo. She also was very ugly and had a face only a mother could love.

But, she must have made up for it in other ways because she was never lacking. She always got her share of dates. My enlistment was up in September, 1966. I got out of the military and returned to Valdosta. My goal was to get a college education. There was no excuse not to because I had a four year fully paid GI Bill at that time. I also would receive pay while going to school. But I guess it was not to be because I found a job and a girlfriend. I got married and started a family.

I do enjoy reading and doing crossword puzzles, two hobbies I think would be good for anyone planning to write a book one day. I grew up with an inferiority complex and was a very insecure person. I still am not out of the woods, but I have made a lot of progress. I have greatly increased my self esteem and learned how to do for myself. Sure, I wanted a college education and could still complete a degree at my present age.

But, I decided to sacrifice the prestige and overcompensate in some other area of achievement. I have operated several small businesses over the years, including the Super "S" Restaurant for over a year and a janitorial service for more than fifteen years.

Also, this is my second book. The title of my first book was, "The Black Psyche in America".

So overall I don't regret anything. My formal education is limited to a high school diploma and two college courses for one semester while in the service. My writing should be raw, crude and pure, so hang on for a ride. I know everyone can't agree with a lot of what I write, but that is what's so great about this great country. Everyone has the right to express his own beliefs.

I have chosen to express some very strong views on social issues. I expect some very strong disagreements. So I wish only one thing to those disagreeing. Please disagree without becoming disagreeable.

THE END